PJ-EAX-599

Chuck and Blanche Johnson's

Savor™
Oregon
Cookbook

Oregon's Finest Restaurants & Lodges
Their Recipes & Their Histories

Wilderness Adventures Press, Inc.
Belgrade, Montana

This book was manufactured with an easy-open, lay-flat binding.

© 2004 by Chuck and Blanche Johnson
Photographs contained herein © 2004 as noted

Map, book design, and cover design © 2004 Wilderness Adventures Press, Inc.™

Published by Wilderness Adventures Press, Inc.™
45 Buckskin Road
Belgrade, MT 59714
1-800-925-3339
Web site: www.wildadv.com
E-mail: books@wildadv.com
First Edition

All rights reserved, including the right to reproduce this book or portions thereof in any form or by any means, electronic or mechanical, including photocopying, recording, or by any information storage and retrieval system, without permission in writing from the publisher. All inquiries should be addressed to: Wilderness Adventures Press, Inc.™, 45 Buckskin Road, Belgrade, MT 59714

Printed in the United States of America

Library of Congress Cataloging-in-Publication Data

Johnson, Chuck.
  Chuck and Blanche Johnson's savor Oregon cookbook : Oregon's finest restaurants & lodges their recipes & their histories.
      p. cm.
  Includes index.
  ISBN 1-932098-06-2
  1. Cookery. 2. Restaurants–Oregon. I. Title: Savor Oregon cookbook. II. Johnson, Blanche, 1943-
III. Title.
  TX714.J5985 2004
  641.5–dc22

                    2004002598

TABLE OF CONTENTS

INTRODUCTION

The state of Oregon is blessed with a wide variety of landscapes, from the rocky Pacific coastline to the rolling wheat fields and sagebrush deserts of eastern Oregon. Those who live in Oregon have a vast playground in their own backyard, and those of us who have the pleasure to visit the state can find enjoyment in every part of it.

This second book in our cookbook series features the finest restaurants in Oregon, many of them located in some of the most beautiful settings that this country has to offer. We have purposely left Portland out of this book. Since the city has so many great restaurants, we felt it best to feature them in a book on Portland alone that will be published in the near future.

It is important to note that all of the featured restaurants were by invitation. None of the restaurants are charged for appearing in the book. We selected them based on the excellence and uniqueness of their food, as well as their ambience. Many have interesting histories. We also looked for places that featured wines; especially Oregon wines.

The reader can use this book as both a cookbook and a travel guide. We enjoyed selecting many historic photos from some of Oregon's many museums, as well as capturing present day Oregon with our own cameras. Savor Oregon has over 125 delicious recipes that you can take pleasure in recreating in your own home. The recipes will also give you a flavor for the type of cuisine you can expect in each of the restaurants, and the map will help you locate them. Get out and experience the best of Oregon's restaurants!

Blanche and Chuck Johnson

Schooner "Hustler" at "The Cave" - Young's River about 1895

ACKNOWLEDGMENTS

We would like to give our special thanks to the owners, managers, and chefs of the featured restaurants for their help in gathering the information for this book, as well as their generosity in sharing some of their favorite recipes with us.

Our appreciation extends to the gracious staff members of the Oregon museums that we visited. They were a great aid in helping us find historic photos to add to this book.

We also want to give recognition to our graphic designer, Mark Woodward, and to our project manager and editor Lynn Kinnaman, for their efforts in getting this project to fruition.

SAVOR OREGON™ COOKBOOK

0   100 Miles

0   100 KM

 **Restaurant Locations**

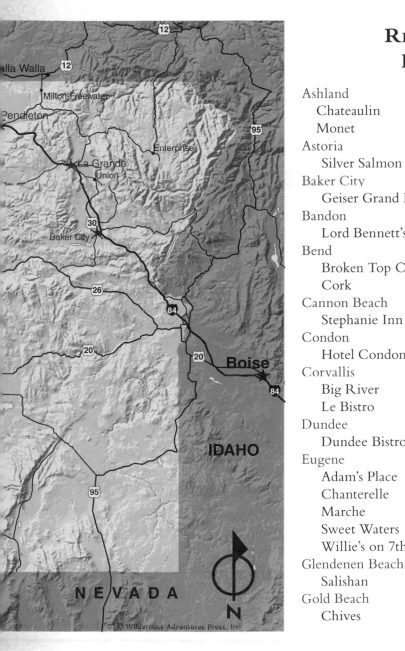

RESTAURANTS
FEATURED

Ashland
  Chateaulin
  Monet
Astoria
  Silver Salmon Grille
Baker City
  Geiser Grand Hotel
Bandon
  Lord Bennett's
Bend
  Broken Top Club
  Cork
Cannon Beach
  Stephanie Inn
Condon
  Hotel Condon
Corvallis
  Big River
  Le Bistro
Dundee
  Dundee Bistro
Eugene
  Adam's Place
  Chanterelle
  Marche
  Sweet Waters
  Willie's on 7th
Glendenen Beach
  Salishan
Gold Beach
  Chives

Hood River
  Columbia Gorge Hotel
  Hood River Hotel
  Stonehedge
Jacksonville
  Jacksonville Inn
Keizer
  Caruso's Italian Grill
La Grande
  Foley Station
Lincoln City
  Bay House
Merlin
  Morrison's
  Rogue River Inn
Pendleton
  Raphael's
Salem
  j james restaurant
  Morton's
  Wild Pear
Silverton
  Rose of Sharon
  Silver Grille
Steamboat
  Steamboat Inn
The Dalles
  Baldwin Saloon

OREGON FACTS

Nineth largest state in the union
    98,386 square miles
    62,966,880 acres
    296 miles of coastline
Elevations - sea level to 11,239 feet
Counties - 36

Towns and Cities - 240
Population (2000 census) - 3,421,399

    6 Indian Reservations
    1 National Park
    13 National Forests
    3 National Monuments
    1 National Memorial
    21 National Wildlife Refuges
    230 State Parks

Nicknames
    Beaver State
Primary Industries
    Timber
    Paper Products
    Farming (Wheat, Cattle)
    Mining (Coal)
    Computer Equipment
    Electronics

*Nez Perce Chief
Grizzly Bear Heart.*

Statehood - 1859 (33rd state)
Capital - Salem
Bird - Western Meadowlark
Animal - American Beaver
Flower - Oregon Grape
Fish - Chinook Salmon
Tree - Douglas Fir
Gemstone - Oregon Sunstone
Mushroom - Chanterelle

Early 20th Century goose hunting.

For Travel Information on Oregon, see: www.traveloregon.com

Chives
Restaurant

Chives
Restaurant

29212 US Highway 101
Gold Beach, Oregon
541-247-4121
866-4-CHIVES

Dinner 5:00 to 9:00 pm
(Wednesday thru Sunday)
Closed January

Rick Jackson in the kitchen.

Chives

Rick and Carla Jackson
Owner/Operator

Chives restaurant is owned and operated by Rick and Carla Jackson. Both Carla and Rick owned restaurants before opening Chives, and their experience convinced them that no matter where you go, people will respond to sincerity and quality. Their philosophy was proven right when they opened Chives on the southern Oregon coast in 1995. The restaurant got the attention of reviewers across the county. Sunset Magazine and Bon Appetite were two that mentioned the restaurant, along with many local newspapers and reviewers.

In 2001, Rick and Carla purchased a house on 3½ acres of grassy dunes in Gold Beach. A woman named Maude Morse had built the 4,500 square foot house in 1946. She used the home to care for and entertain family and friends, and her fabulous holiday parties were legendary. She would invite the entire community, including such notables as R.D. Hume, then a local cannery owner, and Nicholas Murray Butler, the president of Columbia University. Her gardens were so spectacular that the Oregon Federation of Garden Clubs honored her as an exceptional gardener. Fuchsia, calla lilies, lavender, dahlia, dogwood and many other species of native plants enhance the grounds.

It is the perfect setting for Chives. The former living room, with its pegged-random plank oak floor and Douglas fir ceiling, is now the dining room. The east wall of the dining room has a six-foot wide fireplace and the west wall is entirely made up of windows, overlooking the coastal pines and crashing surf. The dining room and the lounge open up to outdoor seating on a 1,000 square foot deck with a fire pit.

Chives serves fresh food from the garden and uses local seafood, cheese, mushrooms, berries, and game. The breads and pastries are baked at the restaurant, and all food is prepared to order. At Chives, Rick and Carla treat you as they would a guest in their own home.

Patio at Chives.

PAN ROASTED PORK TENDERLOIN

with Garnet Yams, Cabbage, Currants and Whole Grain Mustard Butter Sauce

Ingredients

24 ounces pork tenderloin, cleaned	taste of salt and pepper
1 head green cabbage	1½ pounds garnet yams
(¼, hull and slice into ¼ inch ribbons)	(peel, chop and boil until soft)
1 ounce dry Zante currants	1 tablespoon brown sugar
2 ounces water	2 ounces cream

Preparation

OIL AND SEASON pork tenderloin and place in a hot pan. Roast for approximately 9 minutes for medium doneness. Cover and let rest.

HEAT cream and brown sugar in bowl and whip with cooked yams.

AFTER pork has rested, use pan drippings to braise cabbage (add water if needed), add currants and cook until soft and bright green.

For the Mustard Butter Sauce

6 ounces dry white wine	1 pound sweet butter
1 tablespoon white wine vinegar	1 ounce coarse ground mustard
1 tablespoon chopped shallots	salt and pepper to taste
1 ounce heavy cream	

Preparation

COMBINE white wine, vinegar and chopped shallots in pan and reduce by 80 percent.
ADD cream, bring to a boil.
CUT butter into small pieces and whisk in to reduction over medium-low heat.
ADD mustard and salt and pepper to taste.
COMBINE cabbage-currant mixture and spoon to cover the bottom of plate. Place yams in the center of the plate.
SLICE pork into medallions and layer in a circle on top of yams. Pour butter sauce over exposed cabbage.

Wine suggestion: a quality Oregon Pinot

CURRIED CARROT WITH CHIVE SOUR CREAM
Soup

Ingredients

1 pound carrots, peeled and chopped
1 small Spanish onion
  (approximately 4 ounces),
  peeled and chopped
1 quart water

1 pint heavy cream
2 tablespoons standard curry powder
  taste of salt and pepper
  chicken stock or water to thin

Preparation

BOIL carrots and onion until soft. Mix carrot-onion mixture with cream, curry powder, salt and pepper. Thin with water or chicken stock. Ladle into bowls and top with sour cream and chives (or chive blossoms).

Drink suggestion: a cosmopolitan made with Chopin vodka

Dining room, Chives.

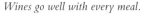

Wines go well with every meal.

CHOCOLATE POT AU CRÈME WITH WARM BERRIES

Ingredients

5 large egg yolks
2 ounces granulated sugar

1 pint heavy cream
3 ounces semi-sweet chocolate chips

Preparation

MELT chocolate chips in a bowl large enough to hold all items. Put yolks and sugar in another bowl. Boil cream. Slowly whisk cream into yolks, tempering. Strain into chocolate and whisk. Divide into four equal portions in four flat soup bowls and bake at 250 degrees for approximately ten minutes. Chill. Warm fresh berries of your choice with a little sugar and pour over pot au crème.
SERVE immediately.

Drink suggestion: an old port

Gold Beach, Oregon.

THE WINE SPECTATOR AWARD

Many of the restaurants included in this cookbook have been recognized by Wine Spectator, the world's most popular wine magazine. It reviews more than 10,000 wines each year and covers travel, fine dining and the lifestyle of wine for novices and connoisseurs alike. Through its Restaurant Awards program, the magazine recognizes restaurants around the world that offer distinguished wine lists.

Awards are given in three tiers. In 2003, more than 3,600 restaurants earned wine list awards. To qualify, wine lists must provide vintages and appellations for all selections. The overall presentation and appearance of the list are also important. Once past these initial requirements, lists are then judged for one of three awards: the Award of Excellence, the Best of Award of Excellence, and the Grand Award.

- **Award of Excellence**—The basic Award of Excellence recognizes restaurants with lists that offer a well-chosen selection of quality producers, along with a thematic match to the menu in both price and style.
- **Best of Award of Excellence**—The second-tier Best of Award of Excellence was created to give special recognition to those restaurants that exceed the requirements of the basic category. These lists must display vintage depth, including vertical offerings of several top wines, as well as excellent breadth from major wine growing regions.
- **Grand Award**—The highest award, the Grand Award, is given to those restaurants that show an uncompromising, passionate devotion to quality. These lists show serious depth of mature vintages, outstanding breadth in their vertical offerings, excellent harmony with the menu, and superior organization and presentation. In 2003, only 89 restaurants held Wine Spectator Grand Awards.

 Award of Excellence    Best of Award of Excellence

 Grand Award

Lord Bennett's

1695 Beach Loop Rd.
Bandon, Oregon
541-347-3663

Lunch 11:00 am to 2:30 pm
Dinner 5:00 to 9:00 pm
Brunch Saturday and Sunday
10:00 am to 2:30 pm

Lord Bennett's Restaurant
Rich Iverson, Chef

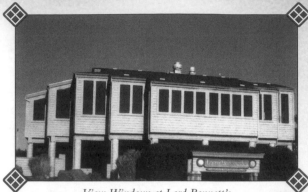

View Windows at Lord Bennett's.

Lord Bennett's Restaurant and Lounge is off the beaten track on Bandon's beautiful Beach Loop Drive. Renowned architect Richard Snapp designed this contemporary beach style building to showcase the unparalleled panoramic 160-degree Pacific Ocean view. For the sunset aficionado or the ardent storm watcher there isn't a bad seat in this window-laden house.

The monolith "Face Rock" and the surrounding rock formations, known as "Seastacks", are focal points. As legend has it, Ewauna, the daughter of Chief Siskiyou, came down from the mountains and waded in the surf, against wise advice. The Evil Spirit of the Sea, Seatka, grabbed the princess. Despite the efforts of her loyal dog Komax, Ewauna could not escape. However, she refused to look Seatka in the eye, knowing it would be her doom. Ewauna gazed steadfastly at the moon, and when dawn broke, she had been turned to stone along with her dog, cat and kittens.

The restaurant is named after George Bennett, an influential Irish immigrant. In 1874 Bennett established the nearby town of Bandon, naming it after his hometown in Ireland. Bandon is a small beach town with a quaint Old Town section and Bandon Dunes Golf Resort. The owner and chef of Lord Bennett's, Rich Iverson, is a graduate of The Culinary Institute of New York. At Lord Bennett's the salad dressings, sauces, soups, desserts, and baked goods are all made from scratch. The menu, like the wine list, is well chosen and diverse, featuring specialty seafood, fowl, and meat selections. Iverson credits his friendly and efficient crew as a crucial element of his eatery's success.

Lord Bennett's is open seven days a week for lunch, dinner and offers an outstanding weekend brunch. On weekends, the Torturer of Tourists Show brings live entertainment to the downstairs lounge.

Dining room at Lord Bennett's.

Lord Bennett's, Bandon

Halibut Nut Crust

Ingredients

5 ounces halibut fillet
egg wash
1 egg beaten with 6 ounces milk flour
bread crumbs - unseasoned

nuts (such as cashews, peanuts, pecans, walnuts)
oil (preferably clarified butter)

Preparation

IN A food processor pulse nuts to medium consistency. Mix one cup nuts with two cups bread crumbs. Dredge halibut in flour, then egg wash and press nut mixture and bread crumbs firmly down so mixture will adhere to fish. Fry in oil on medium-low heat for approximately 4-5 minutes per side.
SERVE with lemons.

Serves 1

Lemon Souffle Pancakes

Ingredients

1 cup cottage cheese
1 tablespoon maple syrup
2 tablespoons fresh lemon juice
2 teaspoons lemon zest
2 tablespoons vegetable oil

3 egg yolks
2 teaspoons baking powder
½ cup flour
¼ teaspoon salt
3 egg whites

Preparation

IN A food processor, purée cottage cheese till creamy. Add maple syrup, lemon juice, zest, vegetable oil, egg yolks, baking powder, flour and salt, blend till smooth. Whip egg whites in mixer until stiff. Fold into pancake mixture and cook as you would any pancakes.
SERVE with maple syrup.

Serves 4

LEMON SOUR CREAM PIE

Ingredients

1 cup sugar
3½ tablespoons cornstarch
1 tablespoon lemon rind, grated
½ cup fresh lemon juice
3 egg yolks, slightly beaten
1 cup milk

¼ cup butter
1 cup cultured sour cream
1 baked 9-inch pie shell
1 cup heavy whipping cream, whipped
Lemon twist for garnish

Preparation

COMBINE sugar, cornstarch, lemon rind, lemon juice, egg yolks and milk in heavy saucepan; cook over medium heat until thick.
STIR in butter and cool mixture to room temperature.
STIR in sour cream and pour filling into pie shell.
COVER with whipped cream and garnish with lemon twists.
STORE in refrigerator.

Serves 6

Famous ocean views.

Salishan Lodge

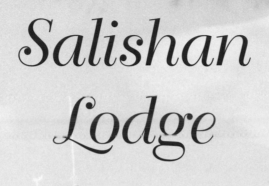

Salishan
SPA & GOLF RESORT

7760 Highway 101 North
Gleneden Beach, Oregon
541-764-2371
www.salishan.com

Sunday through Saturday
Breakfast 6:30 am–11:30 am
Lunch 11:30 am– 2:30 pm
Dinner 5:00 – 9:00 pm

Dining room, Salishan Lodge.

Salishan Lodge
Anthony Pope, General Manager
Seth Rook, Chef de Cuisine

The world-class Salishan lodge offers the visitor spectacular views of the Pacific Ocean, Salishan Peninsula, and the Siletz Bay Estuary. On these grounds, you can play golf on a Scottish style course, play tennis in the indoor facility, enjoy the facilities of the indoor recreation area complete with large swimming pool, or follow the jogging trails that wind through the 760 wooded acres and 3 miles of sandy beaches on the Salishan Peninsula.

After all this recreation, a meal in the Dining Room at Salishan Lodge is the perfect ending to a wonderful day. The restaurant has received the AAA Four Diamond Award and the DiRoNA award. Its wine cellar is a regular recipient of the Wine Spectator Grand Award, with a collection of over 4,500 bottles of international vintages and a tremendous variety of Oregon Pinot Noir.

Relax in the sumptuous dining room with a romantic view of Siletz Bay as you try to narrow your choices on the delectable menu. Some standard dishes are given a new perspective here. Instead of the usual breast of duck, try Salishan's Duck 3 Ways, a combination of a ginger-apricot braised leg, a Muscat glazed breast, and a rich Duck Consommé accompanied by a wild rice cake. Or, instead of a rack of lamb, Salishan offers Medallions of Lamb Rib Eye, crusted with dates and pine nuts and served with a stuffed baby eggplant. The Seared Scallops with Summer Succotash and Sweet Corn Milk are definitely a house favorite.

Warm ambience at the Salishan Lodge.

Whatever your menu choice, the relaxing atmosphere and the fine wine selection combined with a day spent on the Oregon coast will leave you feeling renewed and refreshed.

Y Wine Spectator Award

Molasses and Caraway Seared Elk Loin
With Black Barley Risotto and Honey-Mead Demi-Glace

For the elk

4 6-ounce elk filets
1 cup molasses
½ cup water

2 tablespoon. caraway seed
2 ounces clarified butter

COMBINE water and molasses. In a dry pan over medium heat toast caraway seed lightly. Add to molasses mixture. Trim all fat and silver skin from elk filets and marinate in molasses mixture for one hour. Blot excess marinade from elk, season with salt and pepper and brown on all sides in clarified butter over medium heat. Depending on the thickness of the filet and the desired degree of doneness, it may be necessary to continue cooking for a brief period of time in a 350° oven. Allow meat to rest ten minutes before slicing.

SPOON risotto onto center of the plate and top with chard. Slice elk thinly and fan it out, leaning against the risotto. Arrange chard stems on top and ladle sauce around.

For the risotto

2 tablespoon pancetta, diced
2 tablespoon shallot, minced
2 cup black barley
1 cup dry white wine

1 quart chicken stock
(this amount is approximate)
salt and white pepper to taste
¼ cup heavy cream
2 tablespoon butter

RENDER pancetta in clarified butter until golden brown. Add shallots and cook until soft. Add barley and cook for 2-3 minutes, stirring constantly. Add wine and enough stock to cover. Cook over medium low heat, stirring frequently until stock is nearly absorbed.
Again, add stock to cover and continue cooking and stirring, adding more stock as needed until the barley is fairly dry and al dente Add cream and butter, and season to taste with salt and pepper.

For the sauce

1 cup mead
1 cup honey

1 cup champagne vinegar
1 cup demi-glace

REDUCE mead by two-thirds. Combine honey and vinegar and reduce by two-thirds. Combine and reduce by half. Add demi-glace. Adjust seasoning.

For the red chard

    2 cups balsamic vinegar
    ¼ cup sugar
    1 bunch red chard

IN A small saucepan, combine balsamic vinegar and sugar and bring to a simmer. Separate chard stem from leaves and cut stems into roughly 3"x ½" sticks. Cook stems in vinegar mixture until tender.

ROUGHLY chop chard leaves. Sauté chard leaves in clarified butter over medium high heat until well wilted. Add chicken stock cover and reduce heat. Cook covered until tender. Season to taste with salt and pepper.

Wine Pairing:
A Red Rhone or NW Italian red, such as a Barbaresco.

Serves 4

Dining in the Salishan Lodge wine cellar.

Salishan Lodge, Glendenen Beach

SEARED SCALLOPS
with Summer Succotash and Sweet Corn Milk

For the Scallops

12 large scallops (we use "u10", that is, under ten per pound), abductor muscle removed. "dry packed" are preferred. if you can only get scallops that have been packed in water, blot dry as well as possible. This will help to ensure a nice golden sear.
2 ounces clarified butter
   salt and white pepper to taste

For the Succotash

1 ounce clarified butter
1 tablespoon pancetta, minced
2 tablespoon shallots, minced
2 teaspoon garlic, minced
1 cup sweet corn,
   roasted in the husk and cut from the cob

1 cup English peas
½ cup red bell pepper, small dice
1 cup fresh fava beans
   salt and white pepper to taste
2 ounces whole butter, softened

For the Sauces

2 cups sweet corn,
   roasted in the husk,
   cut from the cob and passed through a juicer.
   salt and white pepper to taste

2 cups English peas,
   blanched in salted water,
   shocked in ice water and passed through a juicer.

Preparation

SAUTÉ pancetta in clarified butter until it begins to brown and some of the fat is rendered off. Add shallots and garlic and cook briefly until soft. Add vegetables and sauté for a few minutes until just soft. Do not overcook or you will lose their bright colors. Season to taste with salt and white pepper. Finish by stirring in whole butter and remove from the heat.

SEASON scallops with salt and white pepper. Using a separate pan, brown well on both sides in clarified butter. The scallops should feel slightly firm. Be careful not to overcook or they will become rubbery.

SPOON succotash into the center of the plate, place three scallops on top and drizzle the corn milk (juice) around. Dot corn milk with pea juice.

Wine pairing: A rich white, such as a German Auslese or Spätlese.

Serves 4

OREGON WINE COUNTRY

The soils and the weather in Oregon are ideally suited for the growing of grapes and the making of fine wines. Oregon's wines are now recognized as among the finest in the world. Pinot Noir is Oregon's flagship wine. Nearly half of the wine grapes planted in Oregon are Pinot Noir. Pinot Noir is a red wine that has flavors of red and black berries and fruits. With aging the wine develops complexity and flavors of leather, tobacco and spices. The other red wines grown in Oregon include Merlot, Cabernet Sauvignon, Syrah and Zinfandel.

Pinot Gris is Oregon's major white wine. These grapes and vines originally came from Alsace, France. Pinot Gris is fruity and spicy. The styles vary from dry and full bodied to crisper wines. The other white wines produced in Oregon are Chardonnay, Riesling Gewurztraminer, Pinot Blanc, Sauvignon Blanc, Viognier and others.

The major wine regions are the north and south Willamette Valley, the Umpqua, the Rogue River valley, the Columbia River and eastern Oregon. There are over 170 wineries in the state. Many of them are open for wine tastings and tours. Visiting wineries is a fun way to enjoy the afternoon, taste and buy some great wines.

The Oregon Wine Advisory Board puts out a great guide book listing the member wineries, their location and the hours they are open for tours or tastings. The fine restaurants featured in this book have a great selection of Oregon wines, make sure you try them.

Oregon Wine Advisory Board
1200 NW Naito Parkway Suite 400
Portland, OR 97209

503-228-8336
www.oregonwine.org

Bay House

5911 SW Highway 101
Lincoln City, Oregon
541-996-3222
www.bayhouserestaurant.com

Winter:
Wednesday-Sunday at 5:30 pm
Saturdays at 5:00 pm to close
Summer:
Sunday-Friday at 5:30 pm
Saturdays at 5:00 pm to close

Bay House
Mollie and Jim Bourne, Owners
Jesse Otero, Chef
Anna Luna, Pastry Chef

Jesse Otero and Anna Luna.

Bay House sits on the shores of the beautiful Siletz Bay. The restaurant is graced with incredible views, gorgeous sunsets and an abundance of birds and wildlife. This gourmet restaurant opened in 1979, and in 1992 Mollie and Jim Bourne and their daughter Leslie Dressel took over the establishment, with the goal of creating one of the best restaurants in the Northwest. The menu features fresh local seafood, organic produce, Oregon lamb and approachable fine wines from around the world. Tom "Mac" McLaren is the wine steward and "Spirits guide" at the Bay House, as well as the keeper of the Wine Spectator "Award of Excellence" wine list. Tom has a keen interest in Oregon wines and is eager to share his knowledge and enthusiasm with his dinner guests.

Chef Jesse Otero designs his Chef's Menu to offer a special multi-course feast for the attentive and excited diner. With the Chef's Menu, the chef is allowed to fully and completely express himself, so this is the format where the kitchen does its most creative and inspired cooking. Jesse's goal for his tasting menus is to provide the diner with a memorable and unmatched dining experience.

Along with the innovations, popular dishes still do remain. The original chef, Barbary Lowry, opened the doors over two decades ago with the house soup; Creamy Onion with Bay Shrimp, and the most popular entrée: Bay House Halibut Parmesan with Lemon Thyme Veloute, and these two items are still on the menu today.

Y Wine Spectator Award

BAY HOUSE HALIBUT PARMESAN

This recipe, as well as the Creamy Onion Soup, has been a Bay House signature recipe since 1979. We always use fresh halibut to make this crowd favorite, and we're often asked for the recipe.

Ingredients

Fresh Pacific or Alaskan Halibut
(4-6 ounce portions)

2 each eggs, beaten
1¼ cups grated Parmesan cheese and
¾ cup all-purpose flour mixed together

For the Lemon-Thyme Veloute

1 8-ounce stick unsalted butter
½ cup all-purpose flour
2 cans chicken stock or broth
½ cup minced shallots

1 tablespoon thyme
½ cup heavy cream
juice from one lemon
salt & pepper to taste

Preparation

MELT butter over medium heat, then add flour and cook for approximately five minutes. Meanwhile, add chicken broth, shallots and thyme and reduce by half. Add cream and return to heat and cook five minutes longer. Slowly add butter and flour mixture. Return to heat and cook five minutes longer.
TAKE OFF the heat and add lemon and seasoning

For the Halibut

DREDGE halibut through egg and shake off excess. Place in Parmesan mixture and press into fish to coat. In large sauté pan, heat oil until ripples form in oil, not smoking. Place coated halibut fillets in pan and sauté until edges are golden brown, flip and place in oven for fifteen minutes or until desired doneness is reached.
Serve over Lemon-Thyme Veloute.

Serves 4

BAY HOUSE CREAMY ONION SOUP

This has been a regular feature on the Bay House menu since 1979.

Ingredients

¼ cup olive oil

4 pounds sweet yellow onions, peeled and finely sliced

3 tablespoons Basmati rice

2 ounces white wine

2 cups clam juice

1 teaspoon dried thyme

¼ cup Marsala

2 cups heavy cream

½ pound bay shrimp

salt and pepper to taste

thyme leaves for garnish

Preparation

IN A large pot heat the oil over medium-low heat. Add onions and sauté until caramelized (dark brown), about 25 minutes. Stir in rice, clam juice, Marsala, thyme, salt and pepper. Bring to a boil and cook about 30 minutes until the rice is very soft. Stir occasionally. Transfer the soup in several batches to a food processor (no more than ⅓ full) and purée until smooth. Put back in the pot with the cream. Reheat over medium-low heat until hot. Add a little shrimp to each bowl, fill with hot soup and garnish the top with fresh thyme leaves.

Serves 6 to 8

ARBORIO CRUSTED OYSTERS
with Lemongrass Broth

We use extra-small or petite, just shocked oysters from our neighbors, the Oregon Oyster Farm. The crunchy texture of the Arborio rice contrasts nicely with the aromatic lemongrass broth.

Oysters

20-40 extra small Pacific oysters
½ cup flour
½ cup toasted Arborio (risotto) rice, ground to powder in food processor

Asian Broth

1 teaspoon pure sesame oil
2 teaspoons minced garlic
½ cup crimini (or button) mushrooms, sliced
1 cup clam juice
1 cup vegetable stock
2 tablespoons finely chopped lemon grass
1 tablespoon minced ginger
1 tablespoon rice wine vinegar

1 teaspoon light soy sauce
2 each diced roma tomatoes
2 each chopped green onions
1 tablespoon chopped cilantro
1½ cups steamed basmati rice (warm)
1 cup fresh spinach leaves
crushed red chilies
salt and pepper to taste

Preparation

COMBINE flour, Arborio rice and a pinch of salt, pepper and cayenne to taste.
IN A saucepan or large sauce pan, sauté mushrooms, garlic, ginger and lemon grass in sesame oil. Add the rest of the broth ingredients through green onions. Flour oysters, shake off excess and set aside. In a large sauté pan, heat olive oil to smoking, then sauté oysters for one minute per side until golden brown and crisp. Add spinach, cilantro and seasonings to broth. Divide into two large serving bowls. Add ¾ cup warm rice to center of each bowl.
DIVIDE oysters and arrange on top of basmati rice, serve immediately.

Serves 2

SEARED SEA SCALLOPS

with Oregon Chardonnay- Clam Pan Sauce and Risotto

This dish has been a Bay House favorite since it went on the menu in the summer of 2002. It is wonderful with a nice bottle of Eyrie Vinyards chardonnay, just be sure to save a half glass for your sauce.

Ingredients

1½ pounds of fresh sea scallops
2 tablespoons of chopped fresh basil, parsley, and chives

4 ounces of chardonnay or other white wine
2 tablespoons butter
¼ pound clams

SEAR scallops in a lightly oiled hot skillet until nicely browned and slightly firm, about two minutes on each side. Toss in clams and deglaze with wine. Continue cooking over medium heat until clams open. Add herbs and butter and reduce sauce till just thick enough to coat scallops. Remove scallops and clams to serving plate and pour sauce over all. SERVE with Risotto.

For the Risotto

4 cups hot chicken stock
3 tablespoons diced onion
3 tablespoons diced fennel
3 tablespoons diced celery
1 tablespoon minced garlic

2 cups Arborio rice
1 cup white wine
4 tablespoons butter
3 tablespoons grated Parmigiano cheese
3 tablespoons fresh chopped chive, parsley, and sage

HAVE chicken stock hot and waiting before you start the risotto. Melt half of the butter in a wide skillet over medium high heat. Add diced vegetables and garlic and "sweat" until translucent, about three minutes. Add Arborio rice and stir through buttered vegetables till nicely coated. Continue to fry, stirring continuously, until rice becomes fragrant and "nutty", about four minutes. Add white wine and stir continuously until most of the wine has evaporated. At this point add the stock, one cup at a time, letting most of the liquid evaporate before adding more. Continuous stirring will produce a creamy textured risotto. Cook risotto till soft yet chewy. Add the herbs, remaining butter, and cheese.
ADJUST flavor with salt and pepper and serve while hot.

Serves 4

SPICY TOMATO SOUP
with Buttered Croutons

This simple recipe is a wonderful way to showcase the flavor of perfectly ripe summer tomatoes. Find the best organic heirloom tomatoes you can and enjoy a perfectly delicious and easy soup. Try this with a bottle of Viognier

Ingredients

1 pound of summer heirloom tomatoes, quartered
1 small Walla Walla onion, thinly sliced
1 teaspoon chipotle chili powder
½ teaspoon cayenne powder
3 tablespoons butter
½ cup cream

For the Buttered Croutons

1 cup cubed bread, crusts removed
3 tablespoons melted butter

Preparation

COMBINE all ingredients in an oven proof roasting pan or appropriate skillet. Cover with foil and roast in a 375-degree oven until tomatoes relinquish their juices and onions appear translucent, about 25 minutes. Cool till just warm and blend with cream. Adjust flavor with kosher salt.
REHEAT and serve with Buttered Croutons.

For the Buttered Croutons

CUT a baguette or other good quality bread into ½ inch cubes. Toss with melted butter and toast in a 325-degree oven until dried and crispy, about 15 minutes.

Serves 4

1897

GERMAN BK. "POTRIMPOS," LONG BEACH

Potrinpus — German Bark wrecked 1897

24

Stephanie Inn

2740 S. Pacific St.
Cannon Beach, Oregon
503-436-2221
www.stephanie-inn.com

Summer Hours: Seatings at 6:00 pm
and 8:30 pm Sunday – Saturday
Off-Season Hours: Seatings at 7:00 pm
Monday – Thursday
Seatings at 6:00 and 8:30 pm
Friday – Sunday

Stephanie Inn

Jan and Steve Martin, Owners
John Newman, Executive Chef

The Stephanie Inn at Cannon Beach sits along the edge of the Pacific Ocean. The Inn, founded by Jan and Steve Martin, opened in April 1993 and was designed to make guests feel as though they were visiting someone in their own home. The interior is constructed from old-growth wood and the fireplaces use local stone to create a rustic ambiance. A piano sits in the oceanfront library, and the rooms are decorated with wicker and wood furniture. The Stephanie Inn is majestic, cozy, and elegant, with the grace of Europe's finest hotels in a charming coastal country setting.

The Inn is pet-free, smoke-free and takes guests 12 years of age and above. Every one of the 46 uniquely furnished rooms is comfortable and casually elegant. Most rooms include a Jacuzzi tub, fireplace, air conditioning, DVD player, deck, silk robes and evening turndown service.

John Newman

In the four-star dining room, the Executive Chef John Newman prepares food with the philosophy of using fresh, local, seasonal ingredients with an emphasis on seasoning, execution, and fundamental cooking techniques. John began working in restaurants while he was in high school. He attended the Culinary Institute of America in New York and interned with the Turtle Bay Hilton and Country Club on Hawaii's north shore. John joined the Stephanie Inn in 1998, and he participates in the annual Taste of the Nation/Chef's Night Out to benefit hunger relief programs.

The dining room offers mountain views, open wood beams, a river rock fireplace and a romantic setting for the four-course prix fixe dinner. A sample menu of the dinner includes Fresh Dungeness Crab Cakes to start, a salad of Artichokes, Pine Nuts and Salsify, and Lamb Chops or Wild Salmon entrees. A French Silk Torte and Vanilla Bean Ice Cream complete the meal.

The Stephanie Inn Dining Room received first place honors at the 5th Annual Chocolate and Coffee Lovers Festival held in Seaside in 2002. This is the third consecutive year that the Inn has received this award. The Stephanie Inn also received the 2001 Readers' Choice Award for the "Best Oregon Lodging" in the March/April 2002 issue of Northwest Palate magazine.

CHARDONNAY POACHED SALMON

In this dish, the flavorful cooking juices from the salmon are reduced and whisked with butter to create a delicious, creamy sauce. Serve with wilted spinach, sautéed mushrooms and a rich, buttery Chardonnay or Pinot Gris.

Ingredients

2 cups Chardonnay or Pinot Gris wine
1 cup cold water
1 medium onion, diced
1 large carrot, diced
2 stalks celery, diced
6 sprigs fresh thyme
2 bay leaves

4 6 to 8-ounce salmon fillets,
   skinned and boned
   salt and freshly ground black pepper
4 ounces unsalted butter (½ stick),
   chilled and diced
   chopped fresh parsley for garnish

Preparation

IN A large skillet, combine the wine, water, onion, carrot, celery, thyme, and bay leaves. Bring the mixture to a boil over high heat. Reduce the heat to medium low and simmer for about 10 minutes.

MEANWHILE, season the salmon fillets on both sides with salt and pepper. Place the fillets in the hot poaching liquid. Cover, and cook until just tender, about 10 to 12 minutes. (The salmon should flake easily with a fork, and should be cooked just through.)

REMOVE the salmon from the poaching liquid with a slotted spoon to a platter and cover to keep warm. Strain half of the poaching liquid through a sieve into a small saucepan and bring it to a boil over medium-high heat. Reduce the heat to a rapid simmer, and cook, about 12 minutes, or until the liquid is reduced by half. Turn off the heat and whisk in the chilled butter, one tablespoon at a time, until the sauce is thick and creamy. Cover to keep warm.

TO SERVE: Place a salmon fillet in the center of each of four pre-warmed plates. Ladle the sauce over the salmon and sprinkle with chopped parsley. Arrange wilted spinach and sautéed mushrooms around the fillet on each plate.

Serves 4

DUNGENESS CRAB CAKES WITH LEMON AIOLI

These crab cakes are pure crab, bound with a light fish mousseline, unlike many crab cakes that are filled with bread crumbs or other fillers. Served with a garlicky, lemon aioli and a glass of chilled Sauvignon Blanc or Semillon, they are the ultimate. At the Inn, the chefs top the crab cakes with a thin slice of lemon and drizzle a touch of balsamic syrup around the edges. The dish is garnished with fresh chopped chives.

Ingredients

For the Crab Cakes

½ pound cooked Dungeness crab meat
2 ounces shelled, tailed, and de-veined
 prawn or shrimp meat
2 ounces fresh scallops
4 tablespoons heavy cream
 juice of ½ lemon

¼ cup fresh chives, chopped
¼ cup fresh parsley, chopped
 salt and freshly ground black pepper to
 taste

For the Lemon Aioli

2 egg yolks
 juice of ½ lemon
1 garlic clove, minced

1 teaspoon Dijon mustard
½ cup olive oil
2 tablespoons cold water

For the Balsamic Syrup

1 cup balsamic vinegar
 salt and freshly ground black pepper to
 taste

fresh chopped chives for garnish

Preparation

TO PREPARE the crab cake mixture, pick through the cooked crab meat and remove shells. Set crab meat aside. In a food processor, combine the prawns, scallops, cream, lemon juice, and salt and pepper to taste. Purée the mixture until smooth. Transfer to a mixing bowl and gently fold in the crab meat, chives, and parsley. Cover the mixture with plastic wrap and chill until needed.

TO MAKE the lemon aioli. In a mixing bowl, whisk the egg yolks until thick and lemon colored. Whisk in the lemon juice, garlic, and mustard, mixing well. Gradually add the olive oil, mixing steadily, until it is incorporated. Season to taste with salt and pepper. Cover and store in the refrigerator until needed.

TO MAKE the balsamic syrup. Pour one cup balsamic vinegar into a saucepan, bring to a boil, and simmer rapidly, until it is reduced to the consistency of maple syrup.

TO COMPLETE the crab cakes. Heat 2 tablespoons of olive oil or butter in a large skillet over medium-high heat. Form ¼-cup portions of the crab cake mixture into small patties, about ½-inch thick. Fry the cakes on both sides until golden brown, about 5 minutes per side.

TO SERVE: Arrange hot crab cakes on a plate and sprinkle with chopped chives. Drizzle a touch of balsamic syrup around the edges and serve with lemon aioli on the side.

Serves 2 as a main course or 4 as an appetizer

Clam digging ca. 1905

Silver Salmon Grille

SILVER SALMON GRILLE
DOWNTOWN ASTORIA

1105 Commercial St.
Astoria, Oregon
503-338-6640
www.silversalmongrille.com

Daily 11:00 am – 10:00 pm
Closed on Thanksgiving, Christmas
and the 4th of July

Silver Salmon Grille
Jeff and Laurie Martin, Owners

As the oldest American settlement west of the Rockies, Astoria offers much to the tourist as well as those lucky enough to live there. Sitting at the mouth of the Columbia River, the area was discovered in 1796 by Capt. Robert Gray on his ship the Columbia Rediviva. A few years later, in the winter of 1805-1806, the Lewis & Clark Expedition approached the area from the east, and built their winter camp nearby at Fort Clatsop. The abundant salmon and berries in the area helped them survive the winter, along with the largesse of the local Clatsop Indian tribe. In 1811, the town of Astoria was founded as a trading post for the Pacific Fur Company.

The Silver Salmon Grille is a relative newcomer to this delightful coastal town, but its location has served as a restaurant for most the building's history since its construction in 1924. The owners, Jeff and Laurie Martin purchased the restaurant in January 2001 and remodeled its interior to reflect it's strong emphasis on local fish catches. The comfortable dining room is decorated with rich wood accents, as well as fish murals and metal sculpture. The inviting lounge features a spectacular 120-year old antique back bar constructed of Scottish Cherry wood. The bar was shipped around Cape Horn in the 1880's on a sailing vessel, and originally used in Anna Bays Social Club, a house of ill repute in Astoria in the late 1800's. It now serves as the perfect setting for a top shelf bar and an inventory of great wines from Oregon and California vineyards, along with some international selections.

While the steaks and other meats are second to none, the variety of seafood dishes is particularly exciting. The ubiquitous Caesar Salad takes several new turns, one with fried calamari and crisp tortilla strips, and another with an abundance of fresh Dungeness crab and Oregon bay shrimp. Salmon is definitely king here, with at least five different entrees on the menu as well as a daily special. The Silver Salmon Supreme is a wonderful entrée of fresh poached salmon filled with a stuffing of Dungeness crab, bay shrimp and smoked Gouda, with a delightful beurre rouge sauce.

Jeff and Laurie Martin have been in the hospitality business for over 25 years. Jeff's experience as a chef at many fine restaurants and country clubs throughout the state has culminated in the service and attention to detail that they put into the Silver Salmon Grille. If you happen to be in the area during the months of February and November, you also might enjoy their Winemakers Dinners. At these dinners you are invited to meet the winemaker of the featured winery, and enjoy the pairing of fine cuisine with excellent wines.

COLUMBIA RIVER KING SALMON
with Dungeness Crab & Green Peppercorn Beurre Blanc

Ingredients

For the Salmon

- 2 6-ounce king salmon fillets, skinned and pin bones removed
- 2 ounces clarified butter
- ½ teaspoon ground pink peppercorns
- 10 Dungeness crab legs
- 2 tablespoons white wine
- 2 fresh dill sprigs for garnish sea salt

For the Green Peppercorn Beurre Blanc

- 1 tablespoon finely chopped shallots
- 1½ tablespoons green peppercorns
- 2 teaspoons fresh dill weed, chopped
- 3 tablespoons white wine
- 3 tablespoons white wine vinegar
- 2 tablespoons heavy cream
- ½ cup butter, cut into ½ inch cubes salt and white pepper to taste

Preparation

For the sauce

PLACE shallots, green peppercorns, white wine and vinegar in small saucepan. Reduce over medium heat until liquid is almost gone. Add heavy cream and fresh dill and bring to a boil for 30 seconds. Remove from heat and add butter slowly, whisking constantly. Adjust seasoning and set aside in warm place.

For the Salmon

HEAT clarified butter in 10-inch sauté pan over medium heat. Season salmon fillets with pink peppercorns and sea salt. Cook salmon skin side up for 5 to 6 minutes, until lightly browned. Turn over and cook another 4 minutes. Place crab legs around edge of sauté pan and deglaze pan with white wine and cover pan with lid. Cook for 1 minute. Remove from heat.

Assembly

PLACE salmon fillet on plate, garnish with crab legs, drizzle sauce over crab and garnish with dill sprigs.

Wine Suggestion: A nice Oregon Pinot Gris or Sauvignon Blanc goes well with this dish.

Serves 2

SMOKED SALMON AND LOBSTER CHOWDER

This recipe was created for the first annual "Seaside Chowder Cook-off". Over forty restaurants from around the Northwest competed and this was judged first place from a panel of chefs and won second place "Peoples Choice" award.

Ingredients

6 cups fish stock or clam juice
2 cups smoked salmon, crumbled to bite size pieces
¾ cup diced onion
2 ounces lobster base
2 bay leaves
½ cup diced celery
¼ cup diced carrot
¼ cup chopped fresh dill
2 pounds rock lobster meat
6 slices bacon, cooked and chopped

4 potatoes, peeled and ½ inch cubed
1 ear fresh corn, cooked and removed from cob
½ pound butter
½ pound flour
1½ to 2 quarts half & half
3 shots tabasco
1½ teaspoon worcestershire
¼ teaspoon nutmeg
¼ teaspoon white pepper
salt to taste

Preparation

PLACE fish stock in 8 to 10 quart sauce pan. Add 1 cup smoked salmon, onion, lobster base, bay leaves, celery, carrot and ½ of the fresh dill. Bring to boil then simmer till vegetables are tender. While simmering add lobster tails to stock. Poach until just done. Cool slightly and cut lobster into bite size pieces. Place potatoes in separate pan, cover potatoes with water and cook until just done. Drain potatoes and set aside. Make roux out of butter and flour. This is done by melting butter over medium heat, stir in flour and cook for 7 to 12 minutes, stirring often. Mixture will bubble and there will be a slightly nutty smell when roux is done. Bring vegetable mixture back to almost boiling and add roux slowly with whisk until completely incorporated. Cook for about 5 minutes, until it thickens.
SCALD 1½ quarts half & half in potato pan.
Gradually add half & half to chowder, whisking constantly. Be careful not to boil chowder after this step. Add remaining smoked salmon, lobster, Tabasco, fresh corn, Worcestershire, cooked bacon, white pepper and nutmeg. Simmer for 5 minutes. Add remainder of half and half if so desired for preferred thickness. Check seasoning and adjust if needed.
GARNISH with remainder of dill.

Wine Suggestion: A nice Chardonnay or Pinot Gris works well with this dish.

Makes approximately 5 quarts

Hazelnut Encrusted Halibut Florentine
With Champagne Oyster Cream

Ingredients

For The Halibut
2 6-ounce fresh halibut fillets
¼ cup hazelnuts, finely chopped
¼ cup panko bread crumbs

For the Spinach
1½ cups baby spinach leaf
2 tablespoons fresh fennel chopped
1 ounces clarified butter
2 tablespoons champagne
salt and white pepper to taste

For the Champagne Oyster Cream
½ cup champagne
½ cup heavy cream
8 yearling oysters cut in ½
1 tablespoon green onion, chopped
2 teaspoon shallots, minced
2 cloves garlic, minced
2 teaspoon butter
2 tablespoon tomato, peeled, seeded and chopped
salt & white pepper

Preparation

For the sauce
MELT butter in sauté pan. Sauté oysters, shallots and garlic 1 minute. Remove oysters and deglaze pan with champagne and reduce until a small amount of champagne is left. Add cream and reduce by half. Return oysters to pan with tomatoes and green onion. Reduce until nice sauce consistency. Salt and white pepper to taste.

For the halibut & spinach
LIGHTLY season halibut with salt and white pepper, mix bread crumbs and hazelnuts, coat halibut with nut mixture. Heat butter in sauté pan over medium heat. Cook halibut until 4 minutes or until brown on each side. Remove halibut from pan and wilt spinach & fennel in butter. Deglaze with champagne and lightly season.

Assembly
PLACE spinach on plate, top with halibut and spoon sauce over halibut.

Wine Suggestion: Meriwether's Capt. William Clark Cuvee or a nice nutty chardonnay.

Serves 2

FRUITED RICE PILAF

Owner Jeff Martin created this side dish for a ladies luncheon at the Astoria Country Club. Any kind of dried fruit, such as pineapple & mango for a tropical flair, can be substituted for the raisins and cranberries. Dried apples and cherries are also nice.

Ingredients

1 cup white rice
1 cup brown rice
½ cup wild rice
6 cups chicken stock or broth
1 medium carrot, diced
1 medium onion, diced
1 stalk celery, diced

1 teaspoon fresh chopped garlic
¼ teaspoon white pepper
¼ teaspoon thyme
½ cup dry cranberries
½ cup golden raisins
¼ cup chopped scallions

Preparation

COOK wild rice in 1½ cups chicken stock. Bring to a boil and simmer until done, drain excess stock. Place 4 cups chicken stock in 2 quart sauce pan with carrots, celery, onion, garlic, white pepper and thyme. Bring to a boil and add white and brown rice. Bring back to a boil then cover and simmer on medium low heat for 12 minutes. Stir raisins and cranberries into rice mixture and cover, simmering for 8 minutes more. Remove from heat and add wild rice and scallions to pilaf.
ADJUST seasonings if needed.

Makes approximately 6 cups pilaf

CHAMPAGNE BERRIES LAURIE ANN

Ingredients

4 cups vanilla bean ice cream

For the Berry Sauce

8 fresh strawberries quartered
½ cup fresh blueberries
½ cup fresh marion berries
½ cup fresh raspberries
(frozen berries can be substituted if necessary)
1 tablespoon butter
1 tablespoon meyers rum

3 tablespoons Grand Marnier
½ cup champagne
¼ cup fresh squeezed orange juice
½ teaspoon cinnamon
¼ teaspoon nutmeg
1 tablespoon corn starch

For Cinnamon Crisp

2 eight inch flour tortillas
¼ cup granulated sugar

1 teaspoon cinnamon
vegetable oil to cook them in

For the Garnish

4 sprigs fresh mint

lightly sweetened whipped cream

Preparation

For Cinnamon Crisp

HEAT oil to 350 degrees in sauce pan or mini fryer. Cut tortillas in to ½ inch strips. Quickly fry strips until golden brown and crisp. Mix sugar and cinnamon together. Roll strips in sugar mixture right after they are removed from oil.

For the Berry Sauce

MELT butter in 10 inch sauté pan over medium to medium high heat. Place berries in pan and deglaze pan with rum (careful, flames will occur). While flaming sprinkle cinnamon and nutmeg over flames into pan. This helps release the flavor in the spices. Add Grand Marnier, orange juice and champagne (reserve 2 tablespoons for slurry) to berries. Mix remaining champagne and corn starch together. Bring to boil quickly and then add corn starch mixture gradually stirring lightly as you add the corn starch. Add just enough to thicken slightly. Remove from heat.

Assembly
DIVIDE ice cream evenly in 4 serving dishes, Wine goblets work well. Divide sauce over top of ice cream and garnish with whipped cream. Place cinnamon crisp on whipped cream and garnish with sprig of mint and a fresh raspberry on top. Serve with a nice berry port or late harvest Riesling and Enjoy!

This delectable dessert was the idea of Laurie Martin and was created by her husband Jeff. A great show if you prepare it in the dining room.

Serves 4

Astoria, Oregon 1886

Dundee Bistro

THE DUNDEE
Bistro
RESTAURANT & BAR

100-A SW Seventh St.
Dundee, Oregon
503-554-1650
www.dundeebistro.com

Monday – Thursday 11:30 am – 8:30 pm
Friday 11:00 am – 9:30 pm
Saturday 11:00 am – 7:00 pm
Sunday Summer 10:00 am –7:00 pm
Winter 11:00 am – 7:00pm

Ponzi Family

The Dundee Bistro
Jason Smith, Chef

The Dundee Bistro is the latest project of the prolific Ponzi family. Dick and Nancy Ponzi founded their family winery and vineyards in 1970, coming to the Willamette Valley from Northern California. The Wine Spectator notes, "Dick and Nancy Ponzi's leadership and quality winemaking have helped drive Oregon for more than 25 years". Dick Ponzi's winemaking philosophy began forming at the family dinner table. The youngest son of an Italian immigrant family, his view of wine was one of family tradition: making wine to enjoy with meals.

Nancy has co-founded some of the most important and successful wine events in the state, and together with Dick, they helped create the Oregon Winegrowers Association and the Oregon Wine Advisory Board.

The family tradition has been carried down, with the next generation working at the winery and also founding the Dundee Bistro in July 1999. Located in the center of Dundee, the bistro features seating in the interior courtyard with views of the surrounding vineyards, as well as fireside dining. The philosophy of the Ponzi family continues in the restaurant, with its dedication to the use of the abundant produce from the gardens, farms, and ranches of the Willamette Valley, using organic ingredients whenever available.

With the history of the family, it is no wonder that the bistro features a wine list of over 100 selections. While Oregon, and especially Willamette Valley, wines are emphasized, the list includes many fine wines from throughout the world. With so many excellent selections on the wine list, the visitor will have no problem finding the perfect compliment to the fresh, local selections on the menu whether it is the Carlton Farms Porchetta, or the Prosciutto Wrapped Wild Mushroom Terrine.

 Wine Spectator Award

Courtyard dining.

PEARL POINT OYSTER STEW

We served this as a soup at the James Beard Centennial Celebration Dinner presented by the Dundee Bistro at the James Beard House in Manhattan. Our version is an adaptation of an original James Beard recipe making use of the excellent products now available in Beard's native Western Oregon. For best results use oysters from clean, cold waters of the Oregon Coast. Ours come from Pearl Point at Netarts Bay.

Ingredients

1½ *pints of oysters and their liquor*
4 *tablespoons of butter*
½ *pint of milk*

1 *pint of cream*
salt, pepper and cayenne
toasted french bread slices

Preparation

DRAIN the liquor from the oysters. Set oysters aside and heat liquor with the milk and cream.
MEANTIME, heat 4 bowls and add 1 tablespoon of butter to each bowl to melt.
SEASON the hot cream and oyster liquor mixture with salt, pepper and cayenne.
ADD the oysters. Bring just to the boiling point but do not boil. When steaming hot, pour into the bowls and serve with toasted French bread.

Wine Suggestion: Ponzi Chardonnay Reserve

Serves 4

CARLTON FARMS PORCHETTA

An Italian inspired pork roast utilizing two of nearby Carlton Farm's all natural pork products. The Italian sausage is handcrafted by Salumeria de Carlo utilizing pork from Carlton Farms. Their pork loin is tender and juicy and is quite simply the best!

Ingredients

1   full pork loin, strap off, butter flied length wise to a 1 inch thickness (ask your butcher to do this for you)
¼   cup fresh, chopped rosemary
1   lemon cut in half
    kosher salt

    fresh ground black pepper
1   head of garlic, split in half horizontally
1   pound Salumeria de Carlo's pork sausage (about 4 sausages)
½   bottle of red wine
    kitchen twine

Preparation

PREHEAT over to 325 degrees

BRING the red wine to a boil. Drop the sausages into the wine. Turn to simmer and slowly cook the sausages through, about 10 minutes.

ALLOW the sausages to cool in the wine, then separate and reserve both.

SPREAD out the butter flied pork loin lengthwise in front of you and rub liberally with garlic, lemon, salt, pepper and rosemary. Lay sausages out horizontally in the lower third of the loin. Roll up the meat, enclosing the sausages in the center. Secure the roll with kitchen twine and rub the outside of the roll with the garlic, lemon, salt, pepper and rosemary.

IN A hot braising pan, sear meat on high heat to brown, add the red wine from the sausages.

ROAST at 325 degrees for approximately 1½ hours until a temperature of 140 degrees is reached on a bi-metallic stemmed thermometer. Allow to rest at room temperature for 15 minutes before carving.

Wine Suggestion: Ponzi Pinot Noir Reserve.

Serves 8

HONEY CRISP APPLE BROWN BETTY
Hazelnut Ice Cream & Ransom Grappa Crème Anglaise

Our Pastry Chef, Kelly Shattuck, looks forward to fall when the apple harvest begins at nearby Smith's Berry Barn. Over 30 different varieties of apples are grown, from the scuffy, intensely flavored Cox's Orange Pippen to the tartly sweet Northern Spy, finely textured Gala, crunchy rich, aromatic Spinzenberg. Honey Crisp is a variety perfectly suited to apple pies, cobblers, crisps and the traditional Brown Betty. If "heritage" apples are not available, look for fresh, firm, slightly tart varieties such as Granny Smith.

Ingredients

For the Brown Betty

- 2 cups challah bread, crust removed, diced ½ inch cubes
- 4 Honey Crisp apples, peeled, cored & quartered
- 1 cup brown sugar
- ½ cup apple cider
- 3 tablespoons unsalted butter
- 1½ tablespoons brandy
- ½ tablespoon cinnamon, ground
- pinch nutmeg
- pinch salt
- pinch cloves, ground
- ½ tablespoon vanilla extract

For the Ice Cream

- 2 inch piece of vanilla bean, split
- ½ cup whole milk
- ⅓ cup granulated sugar
- 1 cup heavy cream
- 1 egg plus 1 yolk
- 1 cup prepared hazelnut butter

For the Grappa Crème Anglaise

- 1 cup heavy cream
- 2 ounces granulated sugar
- 3 egg yolks
- ½ teaspoon vanilla extract
- 2 tablespoons grappa

Preparation

For the Brown Betty

PREHEAT the oven to 250 degrees.

PLACE bread cubes on baking sheet and toast for 25-30 minutes until golden brown and dry. Remove and set aside. Increase oven temperature to 350 degrees.

COMBINE half of the quartered apples, brown sugar, apple cider, butter, brandy, cinnamon, nutmeg, salt, and clove. Sauté over medium heat until apples are soft, about 20 minutes. Remove from heat and stir in vanilla. Let cool. Purée until smooth.

CUT remaining apples into ½ inch dice. Mix together with the toasted bread cubes and apple purée. Pour into a buttered baking dish

Honey Crisp Apple Brown Betty, continued

BAKE 45 minutes or until lightly browned on top. Allow to rest for 30 minutes before serving.

For the Ice Cream
COMBINE vanilla bean, milk, half of the sugar and the heavy cream in a saucepan. Slowly bring to 175 degrees.
COMBINE the eggs and the remaining sugar. Whip until pale yellow and thick.
SLOWLY add cream mixture into the eggs and warm to 180 degrees over a double boiler.
WHISK in hazelnut butter, strain to remove vanilla bean and cool.
PROCESS mixture in ice cream maker as per manufacturer's instructions.

For the Grappa Crème Anglaise
IN A heavy bottomed saucepan, scald cream and half of the sugar.
COME egg yolks and remaining sugar. Mix well.
SLOWLY add hot cream to egg mixture, stirring continuously.

Wine Suggestion: Ponzi Vino Gelato, Late Harvest Riesling is a perfect match.

Serves 4

Dining room, Dundee Bistro.

Caruso's Italian Cafe

Caruso's
Italian Cafe

4907 River Rd. N.
Keizer, Oregon
503-393-8272
Fax 503-856-9230

Dinner:
Seating nightly 5:00 pm–9:00 pm

Caruso's Italian Café

Jerry and Angie Phipps, Owners
Jerry Phipps, Chef

Angie and Jerry Phipps

Jerry and Angie Phipps love good food and wine. Combine that with a desire to bring something unique to the Salem/Keizer restaurant scene, and you have the impetus for Caruso's Italian Café. Caruso's opened in December of 2000 and features Northern Italian style cuisine, which Chef Jerry learned under Italian chef Alessandro Fasani. He worked with Fasani for several years before taking over the chef duties at the Park Plaza Restaurant in Salem, then later Alessandro's in Portland, which he operated for five years. Chef Jerry has also been a chef at several other notable restaurants, which include The Prime Rib Riverside in Salem, The Oregon Electric Station in Eugene and Marco's Café and Espresso Bar in Portland.

Caruso's Italian Café has received exceptional reviews from the local press, and from diners as well, considering it to be one of the finest restaurants in the mid-Willamette Valley. Jerry Frank, in his "Friday Surprise" column in the Oregonian, named Caruso's the best new restaurant in Oregon in the December 7th, 2001 issue. Caruso's was most recently named "One of the five best kept secrets in Oregon", September 2003 and named as the "Best Italian Restaurant" in the mid-valley by area restaurant professionals, October 2003.

At Caruso's, Chef Jerry delights in preparing authentic Northern Italian dishes in their traditional style. A half-dozen pasta dishes are featured, as well as steak and other entrees. Caruso's Table, a fixed price, multi-course meal, offers antipasti, a hot appetizer, salad, entree and dessert.

Caruso's soft lighting, tasteful music, and simple elegant ambiance make it a highly desirable destination for that special birthday, anniversary, or just anytime you're in the mood for great Italian food. Angie Phipps makes sure patrons feel as if they have been dining at Caruso's for years. Her warm welcoming smile greets newcomers as friends and ensures a pleasant and personal dining experience.

Dining room, Caruso's.

Pollo alla Marsala

Ingredients

2 pounds chicken breast, boneless
3 eggs
3 tablespoons cornstarch
2 tablespoons paprika
1 teaspoons salt
   pinch white pepper
3 tablespoons olive oil

¼ cup shallots, minced
1 cup mushrooms, sliced
½ cup good marsala wine
2 cups chicken stock
1 cup heavy whipping cream
   juice of ½ lemon

Preparation

CUT chicken breast on an angle into thin strips using a good sharp chef's knife. Place in a mixing bowl and add the next 5 ingredients. Knead this mixture with your hands until the chicken has absorbed the egg and cornstarch. (no longer runny but not sticking to your hands)   Refrigerate for at least one hour.

HEAT a large skillet with olive oil until smoking hot. Add chicken and brown evenly. Add mushrooms and shallots. Sauté for 1-2 minutes. Deglaze pan with Marsala wine. Add chicken stock and lemon juice. Reduce by half. Pour in cream and reduce by half to a sauce-like consistency. Taste for salt content and correct if necessary. Serve immediately by itself or over Parmesan risotto or steamed rice.

This dish was originally developed for veal, however using chicken has a broader appeal. If you wish to try this recipe with veal, use a well trimmed veal flank and follow the rest of the recipe as is.

Serves 6

LINGUINE CON FRUTTI DI MARE

(fruit of the sea)

Ingredients

1 pound dry imported linguine	¼ teaspoon white pepper
6 each roma tomatoes- vine ripened, blanched, peeled and seeded	½ teaspoon crushed red chilies
1 each medium onion diced	salt to taste
3 heads minced garlic	1½ pounds assorted rockfish
½ cup chopped fennel or	½ pound clams
1 tablespoon fennel seed	½ pound mussels, cleaned and bearded
1 cup chopped parsley	½ pound bay scallops
1 cup olive oil	2 cups fish or chicken stock
1 tablespoon paprika	4 tablespoons butter

Preparation

CHOP the tomatoes, onion, garlic, fennel and parsley. Combine in a large mixing bowl. Add oil (all but 2 tablespoons), paprika, pepper, chilies and salt. Cut up rock fish into chunks approximately ¾ inch cubes. Add fish and scallops to other ingredients in mixing bowl. Mix well. Taste for salt, add more if needed. Refrigerate for 3-4 hours minimum, preferably overnight.

BRING a large pot of salted water to boil to cook pasta.

PLACE clams and mussels in a large sauce pan with the stock. Cover and bring to a boil. Steam the clams and mussels 1-2 minutes. Discard any that do not open. Remove to a plate reserving the broth. Keep warm. Add remaining oil to another large sauce pan and heat until smoking hot. Add marinated fish and quickly sauté for 2-3 minutes. Stir lightly so not to break up the fish. Pour in the reserved broth. Cover and remove from heat.

ADD pasta to boiling water. Stir immediately. Cook as directed on package, usually 5-6 minutes, to al dente stage. Pour cooked pasta into a colander. Add pasta to fish mixture. Bring to a boil and reduce by half while occasionally tossing gently. Remove from heat and stir in butter. Divide between 4 pasta bowls. Save remaining sauce in bottom of pan. Arrange clams and mussels around bowls. Pour remaining sauce over shellfish.
SERVE immediately.

Serves 4

Frittata con Spinaci

Ingredients

1 pound spinach, chopped and squeezed dry	2 cups chicken stock
¼ cup olive oil	4 cups heavy cream
2 tablespoon garlic chopped	12 large eggs beaten
¼ teaspoon crushed chilies	½ teaspoon salt
¼ cup pine nuts	¼ teaspoon black pepper
	½ cup grated reggiano Parmesan

Preparation

PREHEAT oven to 400 degrees.

COMBINE heavy cream and chicken stock in a saucepan and heat just to a boil and turn off. Heat olive oil in a large saucepan until it starts to smoke. Add pine nuts. Toast in oil until a nice golden brown. Add garlic and then chilies. Fry garlic and chilies for 20 -30 seconds but do not burn. Add spinach, salt and pepper. Stir well with a large spoon, breaking up any clumps of spinach and distributing the seasoning evenly. Add the cream and stock mixture. Bring to a boil and then add the beaten eggs. Stir well with a rubber spatula mixing completely and scrapping the bottom of the pan as well. Continue cooking on the stove top, while stirring, until you notice the egg beginning to cook. Pour into a casserole dish and sprinkle with Parmesan. Bake for 40 minutes at 400 degrees. Remove from oven and let rest for 10 minutes before serving.

Frittatas are traditionally prepared in a cast iron skillet, cooked half way on the stove top, flipped, and finished in the oven. This one is a little different, as it is baked in the oven much like a soufflé. It makes a great vegetable side dish or wonderful as a brunch entrée.

Serves 8

PEARS POACHED IN PORT WINE WITH ZABIGLIONE

For the Pears

    4 *pears (not too ripe)*
    2 *lemons*
    3 *cups granulated sugar*
    4 *cups port wine*

    4 *cups dry red wine*
    1 *cinnamon stick*
    1 *teaspoons cloves*

For the Zabiglione

    4 *egg yolks*
    4 *tablespoons granulated sugar*
    ¼ *cup dry marsala wine*

    1 *cup heavy whipping cream*
    2 *tablespoons powdered sugar*
       toasted hazelnuts (optional)

Preparation for the Pears

PUT the sugar, port, red wine, cinnamon, clove, the juice from the lemon and the lemon itself, in a tall narrow saucepan. If too wide of a pan is used, the pears will not get covered by the poaching liquid. Bring to a boil. Meanwhile peal and core the pears, leaving the stem on, submerging them in lemon water to prevent browning. When port wine is boiling add pears. Reduce heat to low and cover. Poach for 15 to 20 minutes. Periodically check doneness with a toothpick. Pierce at the thickest section. You should feel slight resistance. Remove from heat and cool. Pears will continue to cook as they cool. Remove 1 cup of poaching liquid and reduce it by at least half to create a syrup. Cool.

Preparation for the Zabiglione

PUT the egg yolks and sugar in a stainless steel bowl and whisk briskly until thick and a pale yellow color. Stir in Marsala wine and place over, not in, a pan of boiling water. Cook until thickened stirring continually making sure you scrape the sides of the bowl as you go. Remove from heat and refrigerate until cool. Whip the cream with the powdered sugar until stiff peaks form. Fold the cooled Zabiglione mixture with the cream. Be gentle, too much action will deflate the cream. Refrigerate for several hours to set.

TO SERVE, Place a dollop of Zabiglione on a dessert plate, place drained pear upright in the middle of the Zabiglione. Drizzle port syrup over pear and sprinkle with toasted hazelnuts.

Serves 4

Rose of Sharon

405 N. Water St.
Silverton, Oregon
503-873-3959

Lunch
Tuesday– Friday 11:00 am– 2:00 pm
Dinner
Tuesday– Saturday 5:00 – 9:00 pm

Entrance, Rose of Sharon.

Rose of Sharon
Greg and Teryl Graybeal, Owners

The Rose of Sharon Dinner House is located along Silver Creek in historic Silverton. Greg and Teryl Graybeal opened the restaurant in 1996, fulfilling a dream of Greg's to have a restaurant in an old Victorian house.

The dining areas are the rooms of the house, creating an intimate, yet spacious, private home atmosphere. The décor has a Victorian emphasis, with antiques and cookbooks throughout. The main dining room has a cozy fireplace, as does a second, smaller room. In addition, there is a small private room perfect for celebrating special occasions and romantic rendezvous. During summer months, dining goes "al fresco" on the patio, creek side, under the shade of the catalpa tree.

Greg fell in love with cooking as a child helping his mother, and perfected his style by reading, observing, and experimenting. In 1991, he purchased a deli-health food business and expanded it, baking bread and making homemade soups. Daily bread making and soups continue to be a specialty at Rose of Sharon. The current menu at Rose of Sharon features some established customer favorites as well as a selection of new additions and seasonal dishes. The staples include Crab Stuffed Salmon in Puff Pastry, and Hazelnut Encrusted Chicken, and seasonal additions include rabbit, pheasant, and elk tenderloin.

The Rose of Sharon Restaurant offers a charming atmosphere, good food, wine and beer.

Dining room

PAN SEARED DUCK BREAST
with Wild Rice and Red Wine Cherry Sauce

Ingredients

2 8-ounce boneless duck breasts	1 tablespoon balsamic vinegar
½ cup cooked brown and wild rice	2 teaspoons thyme
1 cup chicken bouillon	1 can bing cherries
1 cup red wine	

Preparation

SEAR duck on both sides. Place in oven at 400 degrees for approximately 15 minutes. Duck should be served medium rare.

PREPARE sauce by boiling chicken bouillon, red wine, vinegar, thyme and drained cherry sauce for ten minutes. It should be slightly thick.

REMOVE from burner and add cherries. Slice duck breasts into thin slices and put on rice then add cherry sauce over the sliced duck breasts.

Recommended wine: Marquam Hill Pinot Noir

Serves 2

CRAB STUFFED SALMON IN PUFF PASTRY
with Beurre Rouge Sauce

Ingredients

6 8-ounce salmon filets
¼ cup Dungeness crab meat
¼ cup cream cheese
2 tablespoons butter

½ puff pastry sheet
½ cup heavy cream
¼ cup Shiraz red wine
⅛ cup Parmesan cheese

Preparation

SEAR salmon on both sides on high heat in a little canola oil. Unfold pastry sheet and spread cream cheese on the inside, along with crab meat. Season with salt, pepper and a tablespoon of butter. Place salmon on bottom third and roll pastry until salmon is enclosed. Bake for 20-25 minutes at 400 degrees until pastry is golden brown.

For the Sauce

Heat heavy cream on high heat with one tablespoon butter, Parmesan cheese and wine. Stir constantly, using a whisk, until it thickens. Drizzle over finished puff salmon.

Recommended wine: Marquam Hill Pinot Gris

Serves 6

SWEET SAUSAGE STUFFED MUSHROOMS
Appetizer

Ingredients

¼ cup Parmesan cheese
 8 large button mushrooms
 6 ounces sweet Italian sausage
⅓ cup heavy cream

½ cup chopped fresh spinach
 8 thin slices of fresh mozzarella cheese
 1 tablespoon butter

Preparation

PULL stems out of mushrooms. Microwave mushroom caps for two minutes. Chop stems into small pieces and sauté in butter, along with the Italian sausage and spinach. Add the heavy cream and Parmesan cheese. Heat on high until thick. Spoon mixture into mushroom caps and top with mozzarella cheese. Heat in the oven at 400 degrees until cheese is melted (about five minutes).

Serves 2

Threshing grain 1910

Silver Grille

206 E. Main St.
Silverton, Oregon
503-873-4035
www.silvergrille.com

Lunch:
Tuesday–Saturday
11:30 am–2:30 pm
Dinner:
Tuesday–Sunday
5:00 pm–9:00 pm

Silver Grille
Jeff Nizlek, Chef/Owner

Entrance, Silver Grille.

Stroll along Silverton's Main Street and you will come across the Silver Grille. Unpretentious in appearance, the Silver Grille relies on innovative culinary creations to capture and hold your attention. Chef Jeff Nizlek uses fresh produce from local farms and quality ingredients in his varied menu, and the effort pays off. The Silver Grille is also a wine shop, and Jeff Nizlek works closely with many valley wine makers, so the wine selection is handpicked and the choices are excellent.

The menu changes according to what is available, and typically offers four to six entrees. Chef Jeff presents an ever-evolving menu, with his signature style featuring the fresh and savory cuisine of the Willamette Valley. Chef Jeff graduated from the Culinary Institute of America in New York in 1994, and has added to his experience through culinary positions at restaurants throughout the United States, Switzerland and France. Chef Jeff was featured as the centerpiece on Food Network's travels throughout the Willamette Valley, preparing "Strawberry Rhubarb Tiramisu" and "Roasted Rack of Silverton Lamb en Crepinette" for the show, "Food Nation with Bobby Flay". Bobby Flay's comment was "the food is incredible. It's some of the best stuff in the country. Back on the east coast, we wish for this."

The ambience of the Silver Grille is warm and welcoming, wine specials and menu selections are featured on the blackboard and rows of tempting wine bottles line the entrance. The assortment includes Australian, Italian and French wines, with emphasis on Oregon's renowned pinots from local wineries.

GRILLED OREGON NEW YORK STEAK
with Oregon Blue Cheese and Bacon Butter with Garlic Mashed Potatoes

Ingredients

Have butcher cut 4 steaks to 10 ounces, trimming most of the fat cap

For the Butter

1 pound butter, we use Cremerie Classique, a European style butter produced in Oregon.

8 ounces Oregon Rogue River Blue Cheese, crumbled

2 cloves garlic

1 bunch thyme

½ onion, minced

4 ounces bacon, diced

salt, pepper

1 bunch parsley, chopped

Preparation

COOK bacon until just crisp. Remove from pan and strain out most of the fat. Add the onion, garlic and thyme, season with salt and pepper and sweat until translucent. Remove and cool. Place butter and half of the blue cheese in mixer and beat to soften. Fold in the rest of the ingredients. Wrap butter in cling film or pipe onto sheet pan with star tip pastry bag. Chill.

AT SERVICE, season steaks and grill to desired temperature. Allow steaks to rest for 15 minutes, slice on bias and place over garlic mashed potatoes. Place butter over steak and heat briefly under broiler. Serve with vegetables and Oregon Pinot Noir.

Serves 4

OREGON WHITE TRUFFLE POTAGE

Preparation

1 pound fingerling potatoes, peeled and
   chopped. Store in water
8 ounces leeks, rough chop
8 ounces onions, rough chop
1 ounce garlic, rough chop
2 quarts, vegetable stock

salt, white pepper
bay leaf
4 ounces Oregon white truffles
2 ounces butter
2 ounces cream
1 ounce white truffle oil

Preparation

IN A large stock pot, heat the butter until it starts to sizzle. Add the onions, leeks and garlic and sweat until soft. Add the potatoes, and cook over medium heat for 10 minutes, stirring often, to soften. Add the white truffles and the stock. Bring to a boil, and reduce heat to low and cook for 15 minutes or until potatoes soften fully. Purée in blender, adjusting salt and pepper to taste. Pass through a fine mesh strainer, keep warm. At service, reheat soup. Whip cream to soft peaks and fold into soup. Adjust flavor with white truffle oil if needed. Serve immediately.

Serves 10

j james
restaurant

325 High Street SE
Pringle Park Plaza
Salem, Oregon
503-362-0888
www.jjamesrestaurant.com

Lunch Monday-Friday
11:30 am to 2:00 pm
Dinner Monday-Thursday
5:30 to 9:00 pm
Friday and Saturday
5:30 to 10:00 pm
Closed Sundays

j james restaurant
Jeff James, Owner/Chef

Capital building, Salem.

The abundant cornucopia of the Willamette Valley is the heart of this restaurant located in the heart of Oregon's state capital. Jeff James, the owner and chef, grew up in nearby Turner. He believes in using the local produce, meats and fish for their superior freshness and quality.

After finishing culinary school, Jeff apprenticed under the executive chef at the Salishan Lodge in Glendenen Beach, OR. From there, he moved on to restaurants in Portland before serving as Sous Chef at the beautiful Columbia Gorge Hotel in Hood River. He then went back to the Salishan Lodge as the Executive Sous Chef. His next destination was to the Freestone Inn and Sun Mountain Lodge in Washington, where he served as Executive Chef. While he was there, Sun Mountain Lodge received the Mobil 4-Star Award and the AAA 4-Diamond Award, as well as the DiRona Award. In 1999, he completed a three-week culinary internship in Lyon, France.

In December, 1999, Jeff opened his own restaurant in Salem. J.james is a culmination of all the culinary experience that Jeff has gathered throughout work at some of the finest establishments in the Northwest. He believes in combining the local foods that reach their seasonal peak together, producing a much more intense taste. The long growing season in the Willamette Valley produces a bumper crop of delicious fruits and vegetables that combine well with the local seafood, shellfish and meats.

The restaurant is a light and airy affair, with large floor to ceiling windows and a mezzanine with more dining area. A background of soft jazz music creates an atmosphere for enjoying a fine meal with friends.

Stop in and try such favorites as semolina dusted trout with black pepper gnocchi, crisp griddled duck cakes, or smoked & grilled pork tenderloin with spicy blackberry ketchup and black bean griddle cake. The dessert menu is absolutely superb, making the restaurant a favorite of locals who harbor a sophisticated sweet tooth.

j james restaurant, dining room.

OREGON ALBACORE TUNA

with Fingerling Potatoes, Green Beans and warm Caper Vinaigrette with Applewood Bacon

Ingredients

1   fresh Albacore Tuna loin (approximately
    2½ pounds), cut into 6-ounce portions.
1   pound fresh green beans, picked,
    blanched and shocked in ice water
1½ pounds small fingerling Yukon pota-
    toes, steamed, halved and chilled until
    needed.
1   large shallot, sliced thin

1   tablespoon caper berries
½   cup duck stock or strong chicken stock
¼   cup sherry vinegar
½   pound Carlton Applewood bacon, large
    dice, cooked and drained
    black pepper and kosher salt to taste

Preparation

SEASON tuna portions with salt and coarsely ground black pepper and sear in hot pan until medium. Quickly steam to heat through green beans and potatoes. Plate tuna on top of green beans and potatoes. To make vinaigrette: sauté shallots and bacon until shallots are opaque. Add capers, stock and vinegar, bring to simmer and pour over fish.

Serves 6

*Carlton Applewood bacon is available from Carlton Farms, for more information see Culinary Sources on page 228

Herbed Ricotta Soufflé

Ingredients

2 handfuls fresh basil
1 handful fresh mint
1 handful fresh flat leaf parsley
2 cups fresh ricotta cheese (whole milk)
½ cup heavy cream

2 eggs
1¼ cups fresh grated Parmesan
    Kalamata olives for garnish crust
    fresh ground black pepper and kosher
    salt to taste

Preparation

PREHEAT over to 375 degrees.

PUT herbs and half of ricotta into food processor and blend until smooth. Add remaining ricotta, cream, and eggs one at a time. Season with salt and pepper. Bake in sprayed stainless mugs on ceramic baking dishes for 20 minutes. Top with olive pieces and sprinkle with a little Parmesan.

Serves 6

CLAFOUTI

Ingredients

3 eggs	2½ ounces flour
6½ ounces sugar	5½ ounces butter
1¾ teaspoon lemon or orange zest	½ of a vanilla bean

Preparation

BROWN butter and vanilla scrapings, set aside.
WHISK eggs, sugar and zest to combine.
WHISK in flour to combine.
STRAIN brown butter into egg, sugar, zest and flour mixture.

FILL tart shells with ¼ cup of mix and top with Marion berries or blackberries.

For the Tart Shells

4 ounces butter	less than 1 egg (¾)
2 ounces powdered sugar	6 ounces all purpose flour

Preparation

ON HIGH speed, cream butter and sugar very well, scrap at least twice.
ON SPEED 3 add eggs in two batches, scraping between each addition.
ON SPEED 1 add flour all at once, mix just until combined.
CHILL on floured surface before using.
BAKE tart shells at 350 degrees for 18-22 minutes.

Hop dryer in Lowell, Oregon ca. 1910

Morton's Bistro

Established in 1989

1128 Edgewater NW
Salem, Oregon
503-585-1113
www.mortonsbistronw.com

Tuesday–Saturday 5:00 pm

Morton's Bistro Northwest
Steve and Annie Morton, Owners

Bistro is the perfect description for this small but exceptional restaurant. Walking down the steps to the basement level, you feel you are entering a place that is not the usual overly contrived restaurant setting. Instead, you walk into a wood-paneled intimate dining area that looks out on a surprise courtyard with ivy-covered walls. The abundance of wine racks lets you know that you will most likely find a pleasing accompaniment to whatever you choose for your meal. Seating only sixty guests, you know you will be receiving special attention.

Steve and Annie Morton opened their bistro in November 1989, after Steve's colorful career in local "hot spots" since high school. Steve, an avid outdoorsman, and Annie, a dedicated teacher, worked hard to resurrect the location in West Salem. The basement had served as a speakeasy during the early 1900's, as well as serving as the location of several fine dining establishments in the 70's and 80's. For several years, it remained empty except for the local ghosts that reportedly walked the floors in the late 80's. Together they have created an unpretentious dining spot that makes you feel at home the first time you visit.

For starters, the Dungeness crab and red pepper fondue served on toasted baguette slices is creamy and sinful. Also delicious is the baked Brie with nuts and fresh fruit.

Lamb, duck, pork and, of course, lots of fresh seafood crown the menu. Steve's creativity shows itself in such dishes as salmon served in a beurre blanc sauce containing capers and raspberries, or the grilled rack of lamb marinated in pinot noir and served with black truffle and red pepper risotto. You can order your own heat level in the Penne Diablo, a superb pasta dish with steamer clams, Andouille sausage, with Dungeness crabs, tomatoes and greens.

BAKED BRIE
Appetizer

Ingredients

1   wedge of Brie, 2-3 ounces
1   tablespoon simple syrup (see below)
1-2 tablespoons brown sugar

1-2 tablespoons chopped nuts
    (roasted hazelnuts, almonds, or
    pecans)
1-2 tablespoons dried or fresh fruit
    (raspberries, blueberries, cranberries)

Preparation

PLACE Brie in a small baking dish. Sprinkle simple syrup, brown sugar, nuts, and fruit over Brie. Bake at 375 degrees for 8-10 minutes. Serve at once with sliced baguette.

SIMPLE syrup. Heat equal amounts of water and sugar over medium heat until sugar dissolves. Cool.

FOR a variation, use Amaretto instead of the simple syrup.

Serves 2-4

ALDER SMOKED DUCK BREAST
with Raspberry Aujous

Ingredients

Bone one duck. Reserve legs for other uses (i.e.. confit). Keep duck breast skin in tact. Save bones for stock.

watercress
baby white potatoes
smoker, alder chips

½ cup fresh raspberries
Frambois (raspberry aperitif)

For the Duck Stock

Roast duck bones in 375 degree oven with the following mirpoix

2 garlic cloves
¼ head fennel root; ¼ inch julienne slices
1 medium carrot; ¼ inch julienne slices

1 medium onion (skin in tact)
¼ inch julienne slices

Preparation

ADD after vegetables are brown, add 2 bay leaves and 2 sprigs of fresh thyme.
DEGLAZE roasting pan with Frambois (raspberry aperitif). Add 2 quarts water. Simmer for approximately 1-1½ hours. Strain. Skim and reduce by ¾. Reserve.
PLACE duck breast skin down in a smoker (Little Chief). Run one pan alder chips until smoke subsides. Remove and refrigerate duck breasts.

When ready to serve

PLACE iron skillet on medium heat. Cross hatch duck breast skin with sharp knife, but do not penetrate meat. Rub breast meat with salt, pepper, and fresh thyme. Cook duck breast skin side down to rare. (Three-quarters of the cooking time done on the skin side will ensure crisp, duck skin.) Turn for brief browning of meat side to medium rare. Remove and reserve on work serving plate.
DEGLAZE iron skillet with duck stock and reduce to glace. Add ½ cup fresh raspberries to sauce. Decant and keep sauce warm.
WILT watercress in warm skillet.
BOIL baby white potatoes; drain and toss with parsley, salt, and pepper.
ASSEMBLE potatoes capped with wilted watercress on warm plate. Cut duck breast on the diagonal. Place crispy skin side up. Pour raspberry aujous on the plate and serve.

Serves 1 or 2

Corn and Lobster Chowder

Ingredients

4 ounces slab bacon, diced
2 medium onions, chopped
2 large russet potatoes, peeled and cubed
3 cups lobster stock, (see recipe below)
4 sprigs fresh thyme

1 bay leaf
12 ounces lobster meat
2 cups fresh or frozen corn
2 cups heavy cream
salt and fresh pepper to taste

For the Lobster Stock

8 6 ounce lobster tails
2 carrots
4 ribs celery
1 medium onion

2 cloves garlic
1 tablespoon thyme
4 bay leaves
2 cups white wine

Preparation

FRY the bacon in a heavy soup pot over medium heat until most of the fat has been rendered. Pour off all but 2 tablespoons of the fat.

SAUTÉ the onions in bacon fat until soft. Add the cubed potatoes, lobster stock, thyme, and bay leaf, and cook until the potatoes are tender and start to break down

ADD the lobster meat and corn and heat thoroughly. Slowly stir in the heavy cream. Let sit for at least 30 minutes. Season to taste with salt and pepper.

LOBSTER STOCK place lobster tails, carrots, celery, onion, garlic, thyme, leaves, white wine in pot of water. Bring to simmer until lobster is cooked. Take out lobster tails. Remove meat and return shells back, into the stock pot. Cook, one hour on low. Strain and cool.

Serves 8

Morton's Bistro, Salem

Fennel Jicama Salad

Ingredients

1 medium jicama bulb, peeled and julienned
1 fennelbulb, thinly sliced
juice of one lemon or lime

ground black pepper to taste
1 tablespoon olive oil
chopped cilantro to taste
salt to taste

Preparation

Mix all ingredients. Serve chilled with spicy, grilled meats.

Serves 4-6

Citrus Banana Ice Cream

Ingredients

3 cups whipping cream
3 cups milk
3 cups sugar
3 lemons, juiced and seeded

3 oranges, juiced and seeded
3 bananas, mashed
(vanilla optional)

Preparation

MIX first three ingredients. Add to ice cream maker. Follow manufacture's directions for processing ice cream. When semi-frozen, add last three ingredients. Cure ice cream in freezer for 2 to 4 hours before serving.

Serves 8-10

Wild Pear

WILD PEAR
Catering & Fine Foods

3635 River Road S.
Salem, Oregon
503-589-4532
503-589-4537 Fax
www.wildpearcatering.com

Lunch:
Tuesday–Saturday 10:00 am–3:00 pm
Dinner:
Thursday–Saturday 5:00 –10:00 pm
Breakfast: Saturday 8:30 am–2:00 pm
Closed Sunday and Monday

Wild Pear
Cecilia & Jessica Ritter, Owners
Jessica Ritter & Erika Jordan, Chefs

The business was primarily catering when Jessica Ritter and her sister, Cecilia, opened Wild Pear Catering and Fine Foods in south Salem in 1999. After leaving the Arbor Café, the sisters were not thinking in terms of opening another restaurant, but offering in-house dining in addition to the catering business seemed logical.

The restaurant business grew, and Jessica and Cecilia responded by increasing hours and adding selections. The catering business remained popular, and the sisters relied on their customer's requests to shape the future of the restaurant side. Wild Pear tried lunch first,

Jessica, Cecilia, and Mai Ritter.

and finding success with that, expanded to dinners without missing a step. The Saturday breakfasts are also always in demand.

Housed in the former Roberts General Store, circa 1900's, the restaurant now includes a gift shop and little bar off the patio. The bar, named Karl's Place in honor of Jessica and Cecilia's father, used to be a feed store, and has found popularity as a local hangout.

In the summertime, the garden porch seating offers delightful views of lush gardens. The nursery is operated by Rita Harris, and sells herbs, plants, and garden gifts seasonally.

Jessica went to culinary school in Boston, was the chef at the Arbor Cafe, and her sister Cecilia was the manager. Chef Erika Jordan graduated from the Western Culinary Institute, and is the one who prepares the weekly dinner specials. Entrees include a Three-Cheese, Roasted Garlic and Tomato Pizza, and Grilled Flat Iron Steak with Gorgonzola butter. Lunch is a treat, too, with crab cake salad, quiche, soups, and pastas.

Jessica and Cecilia have seen their business go from two full-time employees, family, and friends, to 28 employees. They are planning to open a second location in downtown Salem; a gourmet delicatessen and catering shop, scheduled for April of 2004.

The Wild Pear crew.

Mushroom Strudel

Ingredients

6 cups sliced white mushrooms
1 finely chopped red pepper
¼ cup finely chopped green onions
1 clove minced garlic
1 cup shredded Parmesan cheese
1 cup shredded swiss cheese
6 ounces cream cheese, cut into chunks

½ teaspoon dried savory
⅓ cup chicken stock
 salt & pepper to taste
 olive oil for sautéing
8 sheets phyllo dough
4 ounces melted butter

Preparation

PREHEAT oven to 375 degrees.
SAUTÉ onion, garlic and savory in olive oil for one minute, then add mushrooms and cook until soft, about 6-7 minutes. Add chicken stock and cheeses, cook on medium heat until cheeses are melted and well blended season with salt & pepper. Let mixture cool.

LAYER phyllo sheets with butter, as directed on the package.
ONCE all sheets have been layered spoon mixture down the center of the rectangle, leaving a three-inch border on each of the folding sides. Using scissors, cut eight equal strips on each side. Fold each strip over, as in a crisscross pattern, securing each fold with melted butter. Brush strudel with remaining melted butter and sprinkle with poppy seeds. Bake on a cookie sheet for 30-35 minutes.

Serves 8 to 10

Spring Vegetable Risotto

Ingredients

1 small zucchini, diced	salt &pepper
4 spears of asparagus, diced	2 tablespoons olive oil
1 cup of peas,	2 tablespoons butter
1 small onion, diced	6 cups chicken stock heated
1 clove garlic, minced	½ cup dry white wine
zest of two lemons	½ cup Parmesan cheese
	2½ cups arborio rice

Preparation

HEAT 1 tablespoon olive oil in a pan over medium heat and sauté garlic & onions until tender, 2-3 minutes. Add other vegetables and lightly sauté until tender, 2-3 minutes, season with salt. Turn off heat and set aside.

HEAT the remaining oil and 1 tablespoon butter in a pan over medium heat. Stir in the rice to coat the grains and cook for about 1 minute.

ADD the wine and stir until almost completely absorbed by the rice. Add the broth a ½ cup at a time, stirring well after each addition. Wait until each addition is almost completely absorbed before adding the next ½ cup. Reserve ¼ cup to add at the end.

WHEN the rice is tender, but firm, about 20 minutes, turn off the heat. Add the remaining ¼ cup broth, butter, the cooked vegetables and Parmesan cheese and stir well to combine with the rice. Season with salt and pepper to taste.

Pass additional cheese separately.

Serves 8 to 10

Big River Restaurant

BIG RIVER
RESTAURANT AND BAR

101 NW Jackson Street
Corvallis, Oregon
541-757-0694
www.bigriverrest.com

Lunch 11:00 am–2:00 pm
Monday thru Friday
Dinner at 5:00 pm
Monday thru Saturday
Brunch 9:00 am–2:00 pm
Saturday

Big River Restaurant
Brant Pollard and Scott McFarland, Owners
Jochen Bettag, Chef

Big River owners.

In 1995, the Big River Restaurant became a reality. The restaurant was conceived, designed and constructed by Scott McFarland and Sebastian Malinow, and local artist Angela McFarland created most of the artwork. Along with Brant Pollard, they opened the restaurant in December to a line of waiting patrons.

The Executive Chef Jochen Bettag creates a seasonal menu emphasizing local abundance: fresh fruits, vegetables, and seafood, natural Oregon beef, and, of course, plenty of Oregon's fine wines. Kinn Edwards, sommelier, prefers Oregon native wines, with special focus on smaller wineries, especially those he identifies as the up-and-comers. Hearth-baked artisan breads are prepared daily and the heavy brick oven produces a variety of interesting pizza combinations.

The building that houses the restaurant was the original Corvallis Greyhound Bus Station, circa 1920. The large sliding doors ran on tracks that are still visible along the front and side of the building, and the old hinges inside are conversation starters. The building served as a car dealership, auto parts store, and warehouse before becoming Big River Restaurant. The wooden bow trusses, arching high above the bar, are another architectural highlight, and the warehouse origins are echoed in the galvanized duct work. The Willamette River and riverfront park are nearby.

Big River entrance.

Brant Pollard and Scott McFarland strive to offer impeccable service, a voluptuous selection of food and drink and a warm, friendly atmosphere, and, judging by the steady stream of customers, it appears they are achieving that goal.

FRESH PUMPKIN PASTA APPETIZER
with Sage Butter, Toasted Pumpkin Seeds and Sautéed Spinach

Ingredients

For the Pumpkin Pasta

1 each 3 pounds pumpkin
(or 2 cups pumpkin purée)
6 cups flour
1 egg

¼ teaspoon allspice
1 teaspoon salt
2 tablespoons olive oil

For the Toasted Pumpkin Seeds

¼ teaspoon cayenne pepper
1 teaspoon curry powder
½ teaspoon salt
½ cup brown sugar
1 tablespoon olive oil
1 tablespoon water
2 cups pumpkin seeds

4 tablespoons butter
½ bunch fresh sage leaves roughly
chopped
salt to taste
1 pound fresh spinach leaves (washed)
1 tablespoon minced garlic
2 tablespoons olive oil
Freshly grated Reggiano cheese

Preparation

For the Pasta

WHEN using fresh pumpkin, cut in half, scoop out seeds and place cut side down on baking sheet. Pour about 1 cup water on baking sheet, then bake at 350° for approximately 30 minutes (Pumpkin should feel soft to the touch). Let cool just a bit, then peel off the softened skin and refrigerate meat.

PLACE 4 cups of flour on work surface and make a well. Add 2 cups of pumpkin purée and rest of ingredients in middle. Knead into elastic dough using more of the flour as necessary until it is not sticky anymore. Let rest for at least 1 hour before rolling. Roll as thin as possible with rolling pin and cut into strips (a pasta machine comes in very handy here). Separate pasta strips with a little flour sprinkled over to prevent sticking. This recipe will make more than needed for an appetizer of four and you may want to freeze the extra for later use.

For the Pumpkin Seeds

TOAST pumpkin seeds at 350° in single layer on baking sheet until golden (approximately 3-4 minutes). In the meantime melt the rest of ingredients in a metal bowl over low heat until sugar is dissolved and melted. Pour the hot seeds into the metal bowl and mix with metal spoon until mixture cools and sugar firms up again leaving an even coating on the seeds. Turn off oven, leave open to let cool a bit. Then spread seeds out on baking sheet again and place in cooling oven, where seeds will crisp up nicely. There will be enough to add delicious crunch to salads or soups (purée of pumpkin).

HEAT olive oil in sauté pan, add garlic and sweat until flavor develops, add spinach and cook until wilted, salt lightly.

MELT butter in sauté pan add chopped sage leaves and cook until butter turns slightly brown. Set aside. Drop pumpkin pasta in plenty of lightly salted boiling water, when pasta floats to the top, drain and briefly rinse with warm water to wash out starch. Toss in sage butter. Place spinach on center of each plate, then place cooked pasta on top, sprinkle with freshly grated Parmesan and toasted pumpkin seeds.

Serves 4

SEARED SALMON ROULADE OVER SAFFRON RISOTTO
with a Chanterelle Mushroom Sauce

Ingredients

32 ounces Oregon Troll caught salmon, skinless fillet
6 cups saffron risotto (recipe follows)
2 cups chanterelle mushroom sauce (recipe follows)

1 tablespoon olive oil, extra virgin
4 each dill sprigs
salt and pepper to taste

Preparation

PREHEAT oven to 450°. Cut salmon lengthwise into four equal strips. Roll each of the strips into a tight roulade, secure with a bamboo skewer. Rub salmon roulades with oil and season with salt and pepper. In a hot oiled oven safe sauté pan, sear salmon roulades (presentation side down) over medium high heat. Immediately place the entire sauté pan into the oven and cook for 7-10 minutes or until desired doneness is acquired. To assemble, place 1½ cups saffron risotto in the center of a plate. Place salmon on top of the risotto, presentation side up and remove skewer. Spoon the chanterelle mushroom sauce around the risotto. To garnish, place fresh dill sprig on top of the roulade.

For the Saffron Risotto

Makes approximately 6 cups

2 cups Arborio rice	1 tablespoon garlic
3 cups vegetable, chicken, or fish stock	1 tablespoon butter, unsalted
1 teaspoon saffron, ground	1 tablespoon olive oil, extra virgin
1 cup dry white wine	½ cup fresh grated Parmesan Reggiano
1 each Leek, julienne	salt & black pepper to taste

Preparation

IN A saucepan, bring stock and saffron to a simmer. In a separate saucepan, add butter, olive oil, leeks and garlic and stir over a medium low heat. Cook until the leaks are soft. Add rice and allow it to sweat for 2 minutes while constantly stirring. While continuing to stir, add the wine. After most of the wine has been absorbed into the rice, ladle ⅓ of the hot stock into the rice while frequently stirring. Continue this process until most of the liquid is absorbed and the rice is al dente (firm to the teeth). If after adding all of the liquid, the rice is still overly firm, heat more stock and slowly add to the rice mixture until it is finished. At this point, add the Parmesan cheese and season with salt and pepper.

For the Chanterelle Mushroom Sauce

Makes approximately 2 cups

3 cups golden chanterelles, fresh (halved or quartered depending on size)	¾ cup mixed heirloom cherry tomatoes, halved
2 tablespoons butter, unsalted	½ tablespoon dill, minced
1 tablespoon olive oil, extra virgin	1 ounces vodka
1 each shallot, julienne	salt & black pepper to taste

Preparation

IN A sauté pan, over medium high heat, add butter, oil, shallot, and chanterelles. Sauté until mushrooms are tender and soft, then add tomatoes and dill. Sauté until tomatoes warm through. Deglaze with vodka and season with salt and pepper. If desired, off the heat, mount the sauce with a couple tablespoons of cold unsalted butter to give the sauce a nice shiny sheen.

Wine Suggestion : Westrey – Pinot Gris - 2002

Serves 4

GRILLED LAMB

with Scalloped Yam and Yukon Gold Potatoes and Cranberry Demi-glace

Ingredients

For the Cranberry Demi-Glace

2 cups demi-glace (see basic demi-glace)
¼ cups cranberry, frozen concentrate
1 tablespoon balsamic vinegar
1 cups fresh cranberries
salt & pepper to taste

Scalloped Potatoes (make the day ahead if possible)
Makes 8 portions

½ stick butter
1 yellow onion diced
2 tablespoons garlic minced
2 tablespoons flour
1 cup half and half
1 cup heavy cream
1 tablespoon thyme, dried
2 teaspoons salt
1 teaspoon pepper
1½ pounds Yukon gold potatoes, sliced
1 pound yams, peeled and sliced
½ cups Parmesan cheese, grated

12 lamb chops (3 per person)
olive oil
salt & pepper
1 pound green & yellow beans
2 tablespoons fresh butter
1 tablespoon garlic, minced
1 sprig rosemary, picked and chopped
1 roma tomato, medium diced
salt & pepper
4 each yam & Yukon scalloped potato squares (see recipe)

Preparation

FOR the cranberry demi-glace, bring all ingredients to a boil and reduce to desired consistency. Season to taste. Add cranberries just before serving and cook for two minutes. They will retain a beautiful red color this way.

FOR the scalloped yams and potatoes, preheat oven to 325°F. In sauce pan cook the onions in the butter until translucent, then add the garlic until flavor develops. Add flour and cook for another two minutes, then slowly stir in half and half and the cream. Bring mixture to a boil and add seasonings. In the meantime slice potatoes (3mm Blade) in food processor and peel and slice yams with same thickness, but them keep separate. Pour some of the cream sauce into a deep baking sheet and layer with Yukon gold potatoes and yams, making sure to pour cream sauce in between layers. Pour all the leftover sauce over the top and press down potatoes to even them on the tray. Sprinkle Parmesan over the top and bake until golden brown 35-45 minutes depending on thickness.

WE like to blanch the green beans in boiling water for approximately 5 minutes. They will turn out more evenly this way. Make sure to drop them immediately into ice water after blanching to retain color. This can be done the day ahead.

PREHEAT the grill (or grill pan), brush chops with oil and season with salt and pepper. Place them on the grill, turn as needed and cook to desired doneness. Set aside in warm place and let them rest before serving. To finish the green and yellow beans, heat up sauté pan with butter, add garlic, then beans, rosemary and diced tomato, salt and pepper.

Wine Suggestion: Bethel Heights – Pinot Noir – Southeast Block Reserve – 2001

Serves 4

PORK TENDERLOIN

with Honey-Mustard Sauce, Roasted Celery Root, Apples and Bintje
Potatoes with Marjoram, Delicata Squash

For the Basic Demi-Glace

¼ cup canola oil	1 each celery stick, medium diced
2 quart chicken stock	1 teaspoon dried thyme
1 each medium onion, fine diced	2 each bay leaves
1 each carrot, medium diced	¼ cup flour

Preparation

SAUTÉ onions, carrots, celery in sauté pan over medium high heat, until ingredients turn slightly more than golden brown. Turn down the heat to medium, then add flour and stir until flour turns color slightly. Then turn off heat and let cool. In saucepan bring chicken stock to a boil, add sautéed vegetables and spices, bring back to a boil. Turn down heat to simmer, skimming off foam and oils that collect at the top. Reduce until consistency becomes slightly thickened (approximately reduced by half). Strain through fine sieve and refrigerate or freeze until later use.

2 each pork tenderloin (2 pounds)
1 each celery root (1¼ -1½ pounds)
3 each fuji apples
1 bunch marjoram (2 tablespoons dried)
1½ pounds bintje potatoes

1 each butter stick melted
2 each delicata squash
2 cups demi-glace
¼ cup coarse ground mustard
¼ cup honey

Preparation

CUT delicata squash in half lengthwise, scoop out seeds and cut each in half again crosswise. Brush with approximately 1 tablespoon butter on inside, then place on baking sheet skin side down.

PICK leaves from marjoram and chop roughly. Peel celery root with knife and cut into thick and short strips (a little bigger then french fries). Quarter the apples, core, then cut two more wedges out of each quarter. Cut bintje potatoes in half, if they are very small, otherwise quarter them. Toss all vegetables and marjoram in bowl with 3 tablespoons of melted butter, salt and pepper. Transfer to baking sheet with delicata squash and bake for 20-30 minutes at 350°. Vegetables should obtain a nice color.

IN THE meantime, heat cast iron pan over medium high heat. Season tenderloin with salt and pepper and sear in the oil until golden in color. Place the tenderloins with the cast iron pan into oven with the vegetable and cook for 12-15 minutes depending on the diameter of the tenderloins. At Big River we serve the tenderloin medium to medium well. If you prefer well done, be careful not to overcook them as they will turn dry.

Wine Suggestion: Ransom – Gewuerztraminer - 2002

Serves 4

Grilled Scallop Salad

Ingredients

24 ounces scallops, 10/20 size, dry pac fresh
4 teaspoon olive oil, extra virgin
1 cups mango basil salsa (recipe follows)
2 each heirloom tomato, sliced ¼ inch thick

8 ounces mesclun lettuce mix, preferably local organic
6 ounces tequila, lime & cilantro vinaigrette (recipe follows)
salt & black pepper to taste

Preparation

RUB the scallops with olive oil and season with salt and pepper to taste. Place scallops presentation side down on a preheated grill. Grill scallops 1-2 minutes on each side or until desired doneness is acquired. While scallops are on the grill, toss mesclun greens with some of the vinaigrette. For assembly, arrange tomatoes in a semi-circular pattern, allowing room in the center of the plate for the tossed greens. Allow the tossed greens to slightly overlap the tomatoes. Display the grilled scallops on top of the tomatoes while the mango basil salsa cascades down the tossed green. Drizzle the remaining vinaigrette around the edge of the plate.

For the Mango Basil Salsa
Makes 1 cup

⅓ cup mango, small dice
⅓ cup heirloom tomato, small dice
⅓ cup red onion, small dice
4 each fresh basil leaves, chiffonade

2 teaspoon oil, extra virgin
1 teaspoon rice wine vinegar
salt & black pepper to taste
sugar to taste

Preparation
IN A mixing bowl, combine all of the ingredients and mix thoroughly.

For the Tequila, lime & cilantro vinaigrette
Makes 6 ounces

2 tablespoon tequila
1 each lime
½ cup canola oil

1 tablespoon cilantro, rough chopped
salt and pepper to taste
sugar to taste

PLACE tequila in a sauté pan over medium heat until it comes to a simmer. Remove from heat and cool. In a mixing bowl, combine tequila, lime juice, lime zest, and cilantro. Vigorously mix contents with a whisk while slowing adding canola oil to create a temporary emulsion. Season with salt and pepper and balance with sugar.

Wine Suggestion: Eola Hills, Sauvignon Blanc, 2001

Serves 4

Fruit packing and sorting — Willamette Valley

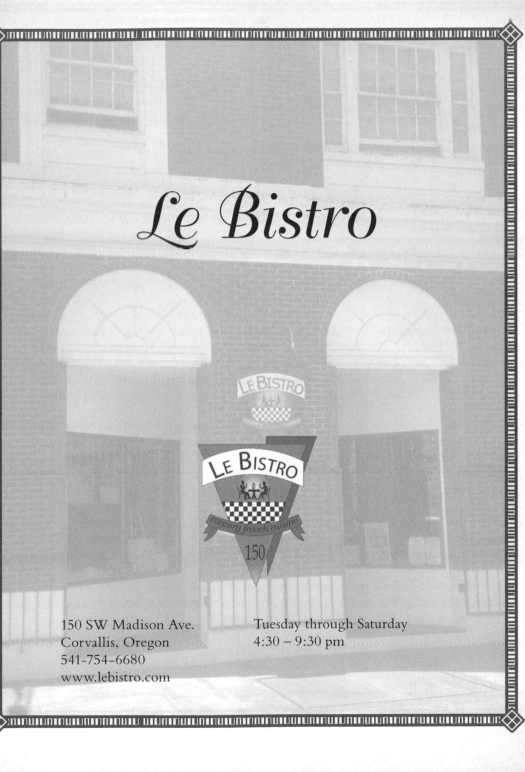

Le Bistro

150 SW Madison Ave.
Corvallis, Oregon
541-754-6680
www.lebistro.com

Tuesday through Saturday
4:30 – 9:30 pm

Entrance, Le Bistro.

Le Bistro
Robert Merlet, Owner/Chef

True French country cooking is the heart of this restaurant located downtown in the former Corvallis Hotel. Built in 1927, the building now serves as an apartment building in the upper floors, with several businesses on the ground level. It is one of the many buildings in the quaint downtown area that are on the National Register of Historic Places. One look through the storefront windows lets you know instinctively that this is a restaurant that you will enjoy.

Chef Robert Merlet opened Le Bistro in June 1998, after discovering Corvallis during a weekend drive. He has a wide and varied career in the food industry. Beginning his career in Paris in 1956, Robert was trained as a charcutier, but was often called upon to cook during his apprenticeship. After a mandatory stint in the French army, Robert heeded the call of the posters in the Metros at the time and moved to the new world via Quebec. In 1969 Robert moved to New Orleans, continuing to create great food, and was soon hired by the Fairmont Hotel Group. This brought him to San Francisco, where he won the West Coast Culinary Competition. Then it was off to Abijan, Ivory Coast in western Africa to serve as Executive Chef at the new Ivory Hotel. After his time there, Robert moved back to San Francisco to help open the kitchens of the Hyatt Regency Embarcadero. In 1973, he opened his own charcuterie in San Mateo, and in 1976 he opened La Gare St. Lazare, which he ran for the next two decades.

Within two months of moving to Corvallis, Robert opened Le Bistro. He says that he loves the Corvallis area, because it reminds him of his native Dordogne region in France. The fare on the menu harks back to the foods of his childhood, but with a contemporary flair from all his worldwide experience. For those who like wild game, his Oven Roasted Quail, finished on the grill and sauced with sweet brandy and orange essence, is an absolute delight. If hearty winter fare is your love, try the Braised Lamb Shank served with white beans. The stock is fantastically flavorful, and the meat literally falls off the bone.

Tourain au Vinaigre Garlic Soup

Ingredients

1 tablespoon duck or chicken fat
5 large garlic cloves
3 tablespoons flour

1 quart filtered or spring water
4 large eggs
⅓ cup red wine vinegar

Preparation

IN A skillet or 3-4 quart sauce pan heat over high heat 1 tablespoon duck fat or chicken fat add five peeled and crushed garlic cloves, brown for 3-4 minutes. Add three spoonfuls of flour, stir and cook for 3 minutes. Add, a little at a time, 1 quart hot filtered water. Reduce heat to simmer for approximately 10 minutes. Separate 4 large eggs add ⅓ cup red wine vinegar, and mix with yokes. Add to sauce pan and bring to the boil for one minute, add egg whites and cook for 3-4 minutes. Salt and pepper to taste. Bon appetite. You may add precooked vermicelli or alphabet pasta if you wish.

Serves 4

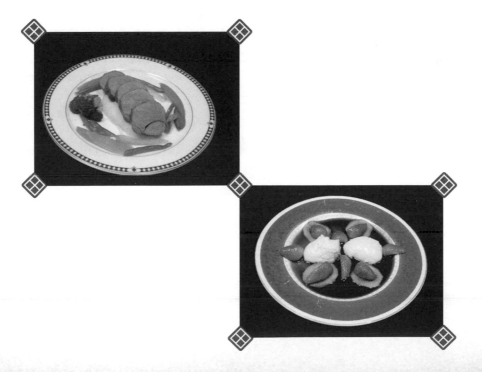

Le Bistro Shank

Ingredients

4 pounds lamb shank
2 tablespoons oil or fat
1 tablespoon butter
1½-2 quarts filtered or spring water
1 small onion
1 carrot
4-5 garlic cloves

2 tablespoons flour
2 tablespoons tomato paste
Bouquet Garni- (celery stalk, sprig of thyme, 2 bay leaves, parsley, cilantro and fresh tarragon and tie together with cooking twine)

Preparation

TRIM the fat from 4 pounds lamb shank.
IN DEEP skillet heat 2 tablespoons oil and 1 tablespoon butter
SEASON shank with salt and pepper
BROWN shank in skillet over medium heat (do not over crust add a little water to avoid over browning) remove from pan, set aside reserve pan juices. Place pan over medium heat. To the pan add 1 small onion; large, coarse dice. Slice one carrot with skin on add to onion. Add 4-5 crushed garlic cloves. Cook for 10-15 minutes Add 2 tablespoons flour cook for 2-3 minutes while stirring add little at time 1½ quart hot filtered water. Add 2 tablespoons tomato paste Make a bouquet garni (put in pan and bring to the boil cover with lid and place in the center of oven at 375 degrees for 2½ hours.

REMOVE from oven and place over a garnish of mashed potato or starch of your choice. Skim the fat from top, and strain through spoon over shank. The lamb can be made 3 days in advance and reheated in microwave or conventional oven. Bon Appetite.

Portobello du Bistro

Ingredients

4 medium portobello mushrooms
4-6 tablespoons olive oil
1 medium onion
⅓ cup white wine
2 cups fresh spinach

1 large red bell pepper
4-8 tablespoons Parmesan cheese
4 slices Muenster cheese
salt and pepper

Preparation

REMOVE stem and skin from 4 medium portobello mushrooms. Grease a pan with olive oil and pour a little on mushroom Salt and pepper and bake at 375° in a preheated oven for 25 minutes.
WHILE this is cooking, thin slice one medium onion and sauté with one spoon of olive oil. Salt and pepper to taste. When onions have caramelized, add one third cup white wine, boil for 2 minutes and set aside. In the same skillet heat one tablespoon olive oil and wilt 2 cups fresh young spinach with salt and pepper. Set aside. Roast one large red bell pepper, remove skin and seeds. Slice length wise. Set aside.

TO PUT it together use ⅔ of onion to stuff mushroom, sprinkle with Parmesan (2 tablespoons cheese). Top with spinach, two slices of bell pepper per mushroom and top with Muenster cheese

IN A small sauce pan add remaining onions, bell pepper, and one cup filtered water. Boil slowly for 10 minutes; blend in blender or with wand blender. Seasoned with cayenne pepper.

Portobello can be prepared in advance and kept a couple of days until ready to bake

Fruit Gazpacho with Coconut Flan

Ingredients

14 ounces light coconut milk
18 ounces milk boiled
10 eggs

14 ounces sugar
2 tablespoons vanilla

For the Sauce

2 cups Oregon Pinot Noir
½ cup sugar
   fresh berries

14 ounces light coconut milk
18 ounces milk Boiled

Preparation

BEAT together 10 eggs, 14 ounces sugar and 2 tablespoons vanilla.
Temper egg mixture with hot coconut milk
MIX all together, skim foam and place in mold or individual cups. Place in bain marie put in center of preheated 350° oven for an hour and a half (adjust cooking time of individual servings). Done when a toothpick placed in the center comes out clean. Cool and refrigerate overnight.

For the Sauce

2 CUPS Oregon Pinot Noir
REDUCE by half over medium low heat, add ½ cup sugar, bring to a boil, and thicken with ½-1 teaspoons corn starch dissolved in cold water

PLACE three scoops of flan in the middle of plate surrounded by fresh Oregon berries (blue, Black, Marion, strawberry), pour Pinot noir sauce over fruit. Serve very cold

Serves – a few hungry people or more not so hungry people

Adam's Place

30 E. Broadway
Eugene, Oregon
541-344-6948
541-344-1266 Fax

Open at 4:00 pm Tuesday – Saturday
Dinner seating ends 8:45 pm
Tuesday – Thursday and 9:45 pm
Friday & Saturday
Available on Sunday & Monday for
private parties and special events

Adam's Place
Adam Bernstein, Owner

Musicians performing in Luna.

Adam Bernstein had twenty years of restaurant experience when he opened Adam's Place in the former Broadway Department Store in Eugene. The main dining room used to be the women's lingerie department, but you'd never know it after the extensive renovation that transformed the old department store into an upscale, elegant restaurant. The mahogany interior, created by designers from New York and San Diego, is reminiscent of the great old hotels of the past. Adam's Place was created to reflect the personal culinary tastes and service standards of its owner and namesake.

Everything from the glassware to the china pattern was painstakingly selected to meet criteria set by Bernstein. The china pattern, Rosemailing, by Homer Laughlen, required numerous trips across country before it was selected and approved. The silver for the first and last course are standard weight and size, but the main course is served with silver that is oversized and extra heavy to bring focus to the entrée. The same level of care went into the décor. While many restaurants today base their selection strictly on appearance, or even deliberately select uncomfortable furniture to encourage frequent turnover, Adam's Place is designed to help guests to relax and enjoy the companionship of family and friends. The framed tapestries, thick carpet, cotton napery, and upholstered chairs were chosen to eliminate excessive sounds and the result is a pleasant environment for leisurely dining and private conversations.

Private dining room, Adam's Place.

Adam's Place seasonal menu features local organic produce, meats and seafood, complemented by a 200 bottle wine list that was awarded the Wine Spectator Award of Excellence. The wine selections showcase Oregon, Northern California, and Washington wines, as well as some from around the world. The restaurant also hosts wine maker dinners, which match outstanding wines with exceptional cuisine. In addition to a great wine list, the "Mahogony Room", the restaurant's pub, boasts an outstanding martini list (the Eugene Martini Association meets here regularly) and has the second largest single malt scotch selection in the Pacific Northwest. Next door to Adam's Place is Luna, Adam Bernstein's intimate jazz club and tapas bar.

 Wine Spectator Award

Adam's Place, Eugene

CHICKEN PICCATA A LA MILANESE

Ingredients

4 eggs, beaten
½ cup grated Parmesan cheese
3 tablespoons chives, chopped
4 chicken breast, boneless & skinless
1 package linguine, cooked
2 tablespoons shallot, chopped

2 tablespoons lemon juice
½ cup white wine
1 cup heavy cream
8 ounces butter
1 cup flour
2 tablespoons caper berries, sliced

Preparation

COMBINE the eggs, Parmesan and chives, then mix to form a batter. dip the chicken Into the flour, dust off excess flour then dip into the egg batter. Oil a pan on medium-low heat and place the chicken in the pan and brown on both sides. Finish the chicken in the oven. While the chicken is cooking beat a saucepan to medium heat and add the shallots, lemon Juice and wine to reduce. When the liquid is half gone, add the cream and reduce to thicken. Finish the sauce by whisking in the butter and, last but not least, add the caper berries. When the chicken is done place on top of your cooked linguine and spoon your sauce over it. ENJOY

Serves 4

PURÉE OF PUMPKIN SOUP

EASY AND YUMMY!!!! You can serve this soup in hollowed out and roasted baby pumpkins for a great presentation, finished with a drizzle of pumpkin seed oil and goat cheese.

Ingredients

1 full can of pumpkin purée
3 quarts vegetable stock
3 cups ½ & ½ milk
3 cloves garlic, minced
¾ cup maple syrup

1½ teaspoons Chinese five spice
3 tablespoons butter
salt and pepper, to taste
1 tablespoon pumpkin seed oil, to taste
1 teaspoon goat cheese

Preparation

MIX the first four ingredients in a pot and bring to a boil, then add the remaining ingredients and simmer until the flavors the have come together (about 15-20 minutes)

Mohogany room, Adam's Place.

CHOCOLATE VOLCANO

Ingredients

24 ounces butter
36 ounces chocolate
12 each egg
12 each egg yolk

1½ cups sugar
½ teaspoon salt
1½ teaspoons cinnamon
¾ cup flour

Preparation

IN THE microwave met the butter and chocolate set aside. In a electric mixer bowl mix the next 5 ingredients at high speed until thickened and white. This takes 10-15 minutes. (per bowl) and you will have to divide the mixture into 2 bowls so it doesn't overflow. Place all the egg mixture into a large stainless steel mixing bowl. Sift flour over egg mixture and fold in followed with the chocolate mixture. Fold gently until blended. Refrigerate.

BUTTER and sugar a soufflé pan shaped like a volcano and scoop 3 healthy scoops of the batter and then bake at 400 degrees for 30 minutes. Unmold onto a plate and, dust with powdered sugar and serve with creme anglaise.

Serves 1

Dining room

Fishing party on Cow Creek — 1910.

Chanterelle

Chanterelle

since 1984

207 E. 5th, Suite 109
Eugene, Oregon
541-484-4065

Dinner 5:00 pm – 10:00 pm
Tuesday thru Saturday

Dining room, Chanterelle.

Chanterelle
Ralf Schmidt, Owner/Operator

Chanterelle opened in 1984 in a building that had been constructed in 1929 and used as a warehouse. The building was renovated in 1981 and again in 2000, after being purchased by Jenova Land Company.

Chanterelle is owned and operated by German-born Ralf Schmidt, who also serves as chef. Schmidt has been in the restaurant business since 1959. The restaurant is small and intimate, with only 13 tables. Appetizers such as Scallops Seviche, Oysters Rockefeller, and Escargots Bourguignon begin the evening. Entree items include Rack of Lamb Provencal, Sautéed Prawns Maison, Zwiebelsteak, and Coquille St. Jacques. The Game of the Week alternates, and prior selections include pheasant, buffalo, and emu. Desserts are created by Schmidt's wife, Gisela, and, according to Schmidt, the restaurant is famous for tiramisu and French Silk pie.

The restaurant's namesake, the Chanterelle mushroom, is the state mushroom of Oregon since 1999. The yellow-orange mushrooms have a fruity fragrance and chewy texture, and the Pacific golden chanterelle is unique to the Pacific Northwest. Over 500,000 pounds of Pacific golden chanterelles are harvested each year, making up a substantial segment of Oregon's commercial mushroom business.

Chanterelle is a non-smoking restaurant and has wine, beer, and a full bar.

Ralf Schmidt, owner.

CHANTERELLE MUSHROOMS
Appetizer

Ingredients

12 ounces fresh chanterelle mushrooms, cleaned and cut bite sized
2 ounces butter
1 garlic clove, chopped
1 strip bacon, finely diced

1 ounces finely chopped onion
2 ounces white wine
   salt, pepper to taste
   pinch of cayenne pepper

Preparation

Sauté bacon at medium heat, add onions until transparent, add garlic and butter. Add mushrooms and turn to high heat. Sauté for one minute remove chanterelles and reduce the natural stock. Return mushrooms. add white wine and cook for 1 minute.

Sauvignon Blanc or Pinot Gris goes well with this dish.

Serves 4

SPAETZLE

Ingredients

3 eggs, extra large
12 ounces flour
1 ounce salad oil
6 ounces cold water

1 ounce salt
   pinch of ground white pepper and nutmeg

Preparation

BEAT eggs, oil and water and seasonings in large bowl. Mix well. Stir in flour slowly until mixture is smooth.
BEAT dough until air bubbles appear. Let rest for 15 minutes. In large pot bring approximately 2 gallons of water to a boil, add enough salt to water to give it a salty taste. Place dough into spaetzle maker over the boiling water and let the spaetzle drop into the water. When spaetzle rise to top drain spaetzle. Lightly sauté pasta in butter.

Serves 4

Chanterelle, Eugene

French Onion Soup Au Gratin
Appetizer

Ingredients For Soup

2 medium onions, sliced
2 tablespoons oil
1 garlic clove, chopped
3 ounces dry sherry or white wine
4 cups chicken broth

Spice bag:
½ ounces peppercorns, crushed
1 ounces whole cloves
¼ teaspoon thyme
1 bay leaf

Ingredients For Au Gratin

4 toasted croutons 3 inches in diameter
5 ounces mozzarella cheese

4 ounces Swiss cheese, grated
5 ounces American cheese, grated

Preparation

PLACE spices in cheese cloth tied into a small bag.

SAUTÉ onions in oil over medium heat until transparent. Add garlic and wine and simmer until reduced to minimum. Add chicken broth and spice bag, simmer 15 minutes. Season to taste with salt. Remove spice bag when broth is seasoned to your taste. Pour into 4 oven proof soup crocks. Top with toasted croutons and sprinkle with mixture of cheeses. Place under broiler until cheese is golden brown.

Serves 4

RACK OF LAMB PROVENCALE

Ingredients

4 whole frenched New Zealand Rack of
   Lamb
2 ounces pepper jelly
2 ounces malaga green peppercorns
   crushed

6 ounces brown sauce
   Dijon mustard
   seasoned bread crumbs
   (garlic,parsley,cajun spice)

Preparation

Season lamb, place in preheated sauté pan meat side down. Put in oven at 425 degrees for 5 minutes, turn over to bone side for another 5 minutes. Remove from oven, take lamb out of pan. Brush meat side with dijon mustard lightly, place this side in the seasoned bread crumbs, remove. Drain ¾ of the fat in the sauté pan, add brown sauce, peppercorns, jelly and 2 ounces of water to pan. Return lamb to pan, meat side up and return to oven for approximately 1 minute or until bread crumbs are golden brown. Remove lamb from pan and reduce sauce. A Petite Syra or a Cabernet Sauvignon complement this wonderful dish.

Serves 4

Mahi Mahi Macadamia Nut

Ingredients

4 8-ounce Mahi Mahi filets	3 ounce white wine
3 ounce crushed macadamia nuts	2 eggs
2½ ounce butter	flour, salt and pepper, 2 ounces oil

Preparation

BEAT eggs. Season Mahi Mahi to taste and dust with flour. Place in egg wash from both sides. Preheat pan with oil and sauté fish quickly from both sides until sealed. Place pan in preheated oven at 425 degrees for approximately 4 minutes, turning fish once during cooking. Remove from oven, drain oil from pan. Place fish on paper towel. Add butter, nuts and white wine to pan, add fish and return to oven for about one more minute or until nuts are golden brown. Place fish on a plate ladle butternut sauce over fish.

A dry Chardonnay or dry German Riesling complement this dish.

Serves 4

Marché

Marché

296 E. Fifth Ave.
Eugene, Oregon
541-342-3612
www.marcherestaurant.com

Monday–Thursday
11:30 am–11:00 pm
Friday–Saturday
11:30 am–midnight
Sunday
10:00 am–11:00 pm

Marché
Stephanie Pearl Kimmel, Executive Chef/Owner

Management team.

The bustling Fifth Street Market in Eugene offers a plethora of dinging establishments, but the Marché stands out from the crowd with its French-based cuisine and dedication to using organic, free range and chemical free ingredients, selected from local markets. The floor to ceiling windows look out on a patio replete with umbrella tables surrounded by a wall of plants and flowers. In the summer the stately lavender is stunning. Inside, a counter on which the day's desserts are displayed surrounds the exhibition kitchen featuring a beautiful wood-fired oven. Anyone strolling by this counter is sure to remember to save room at the end of the meal to sample one of these delicacies.

Stephanie Pearl Kimmel, the Executive Chef and owner, grew up living and traveling around the world. Her father, a career Air Force Pilot, was stationed in Japan, Europe and North Africa, as well as many regions of the United States. Stephanie's formal education was in English Literature and French Cultural History, with degrees from the University of Oregon and the Sorbonne. In 1972, she opened the Excelsior Café in Eugene. At the time the Oregon wine industry was just beginning to bloom, and Stephanie was one of the first to feature these wines in her restaurant. After selling the restaurant in 1993, she took an extended trip to France, which further sharpened her focus on market-oriented cooking.

In the 90's, Stephanie worked with the King Estate Winery to develop an intense culinary department. This resulted in her compiling and editing two cookbooks for the winery: the "King Estate Pinot Gris Cookbook" and the "King Estate Pinot Noir Cookbook". Stephanie was also the Culinary Director of a 13-part cooking series called New American Cuisine, shown nationwide on public television stations.

At Marché. Stephanie has coalesced her worldwide experiences to create an atmosphere that is warm, friendly and elegant. Her Chef de Cuisine, Rocky Maselli, has a background in French and Italian cuisine, after working as Sous Chef for the superb French hotel company, Sofitel, and as the Executive Sous Chef for Il Fornaio with restaurants in California, Oregon and Washington.

Your experience at Marché, whether in the more casual Café or in the elegant dining room, will make

Marché, Eugene

Marché bar.

ROASTED PORTOBELLO MUSHROOM SANDWICH
with Sun Dried Tomato Relish and Herb Aïoli

This is one of the most popular items on our lunch menu—a vegetarian option that is light but has great depth of flavor. The bread is a flat bread we make from pizza dough rolled out and cooked on our grill. You may substitute purchased flat bread.

Ingredients

Mushrooms

1 pound portobello mushrooms (about 4-5 large)	3 tablespoons good quality olive oil
	1 tablespoon salt
	1 teaspoon freshly ground black pepper

Sun Dried Tomato Relish

1 small onion, cut into julienne	¼ cup balsamic vinegar
8 ounces sun dried tomato, cut into julienne	1 teaspoon salt
	¼ teaspoon freshly ground black pepper

Aïoli

1 egg yolk	1 cup good quality olive oil
1 clove garlic, minced	1 teaspoon chopped fresh herbs (parsley, chervil, chives or tarragon
½ teaspoon fresh lemon juice	

4 pizza bread rounds or other flat bread
8 ounces Sonoma Dry Jack cheese, sliced
(or substitute any good melting cheese)

Preparation

To prepare the mushrooms
PREHEAT oven to 350°.
GENTLY brush mushrooms to remove any dirt or debris. Remove stems by slowly twisting them away from the cap.
LAY mushrooms in a single layer on a baking sheet.
BRUSH the mushrooms with olive oil and season with salt and pepper.
ROAST for 25-35 minutes, or until mushrooms do not spring back to the touch.
REMOVE from sheet tray and reserve.

To prepare the relish
(makes about 2 cups and will keep well in the refrigerator)
GENTLY sweat onion in a pan large enough to hold all ingredients.
ADD tomato and heat through.

DEGLAZE with vinegar, reduce heat and cook until vinegar has slightly reduced and tomatoes have softened.

SEASON with salt and pepper.

To prepare the aïoli
(makes about a cup)

PLACE first three ingredients in the bowl of a small food processor.

WITH machine running, add olive oil in a slow, steady stream.

CONTINUE adding oil until aïoli is very thick and smooth.

SEASON to taste with salt and fresh black pepper.

To assemble

PORTION pizza dough into 5 ounce portions.

ROLL into 8" rounds, brush with olive oil and quickly grill over medium heat. (Eliminate the first 2 steps if using purchased bread.)

LAY portobellos on a sheet tray and top with a firm, mild cheese such as Monterey Jack (we use Sonoma Dry Jack), mozzarella, or mild cheddar.

RETURN mushrooms to oven until cheese is melted and mushrooms are heated through.

SPREAD flat bread with a tablespoon of aïoli and cut in half.

PLACE two pieces of mushroom on one side of flat bread, top with two tablespoons of relish and cover with second piece of flat bread.

CUT each sandwich into three triangles.

SERVE with a small green salad.

Serves 8

DUNGENESS CRAB CAKES
with Curry Aïoli and Apple-Ginger Chutney

Ingredients

8 ounces fresh cod filet,
cut into small dice
1 pound fresh crab meat, picked clean
½ cup homemade or good quality
purchased mayonnaise
½ cup thinly sliced green onion,
green part included

1 tablespoon fresh lemon juice
zest of ½ lemon
½ teaspoon salt
¼ teaspoon cayenne
1¼ cups fresh French bread crumbs
butter for sauté pan

Preparation

PUT all ingredients except bread crumbs in a large bowl and gently mix until thoroughly combined. Divide the mixture into 12 portions and flatten into a patty shape.

POUR the bread crumbs into a small baking dish. Lay the crab cakes in the crumbs to coat on both sides. The cakes can be made up to this point and held in the refrigerator for several hours.

JUST before you are ready to serve, heat a couple of tablespoons of unsalted butter in a sauté pan, then brown the crab cakes on each side. Allow to drain on a paper towel and keep warm in a very low oven until all the cakes are finished. Serve hot.

For the Curry Aïoli

½ teaspoon curry powder
2 teaspoons lemon juice
1 cup homemade mayonnaise

To make curry aïoli, make a paste of ½ teaspoon curry powder and 2 teaspoons lemon juice and add to a cup of homemade mayonnaise or a good quality purchased version.

For the Apple Ginger Chutney
For 2 Cups

- 3 apples
- ¼ cup white wine vinegar
- ½ cup brown sugar
- ½ lemon, very thinly sliced, seeded, then chopped
- 1 tablespoon finely chopped fresh ginger
- ¼ cup raisins
- ¼ cup golden raisins
- ¼ teaspoon salt

COMBINE all ingredients in a heavy saucepan and simmer over low heat, stirring from time to time, until apples are golden and translucent and the mixture has thickened. This will take about 45 minutes. Add a little apple juice or water if the mixture starts to stick.

Serves 4

Dining room, Marché.

ROASTED SALMON
with Sorrel Beurre Blanc

Sorrel, a lemony perennial herb, appears in the garden in early spring. It's usually available in the specialty herb section of produce departments or at the Farmers' Market.

Ingredients

- *1   large shallot, minced (you may substitute the white part of a scallion)*
- *½   cup white wine*
- *1   cup heavy cream*
- *4   large sorrel leaves*

- *3   tablespoons cold unsalted butter, cut into ½-inch cubes*
- *4   6-ounce wild salmon filets, preferably center-cut*
- *olive oil*
- *salt and freshly ground pepper*

Preparation

PREHEAT the oven to 425 degrees.

MAKE the sorrel beurre blanc: Combine the minced shallot and white wine in a small non-reactive saucepan. Cook over medium high heat until the liquid is reduced to about a teaspoon. Add the cream and reduce further until quite thick (about the consistency of maple syrup). While the cream mixture is reducing, remove the ribs from the sorrel leaves and cut them into a chiffonade by rolling them and cutting cross wise into thin ribbons. Stir the sorrel into the reduced cream, add the cold butter, and blend until smooth using a hand-held blender, a blender or a food processor. Hold the sauce over warm water on the stove while you prepare the salmon.

DRIZZLE the salmon filets with a little olive oil to coat them, then salt and pepper them generously. Place on a baking sheet and roast in the oven for 8 to 10 minutes, depending on the size of the filets and personal preference.

REMOVE the salmon filets to dinner plates and spoon the sorrel beurre blanc over the top. We serve the dish with chive-mashed potatoes and spring vegetables such as asparagus, fava beans or peas.

Serves 4

HEIRLOOM TOMATO SALAD
with Arugula, Rogue Valley Blue Cheese
and Sherry Vinaigrette

This well-balanced salad is a great choice for a late summer menu. Sweet heirloom tomatoes are at their peak of ripeness and your palate is starting to long for the richer flavors of fall.

Ingredients

1 pound ripe heirloom tomatoes, preferably a mix of shapes and colors
6 ounces small, young arugula leaves

¼ pound blue cheese from Oregon's Rogue Valley Creamery (or substitute another salty, full-flavored blue-veined cheese), crumbled
Freshly ground black pepper

For the Sherry Vinaigrette

1 medium shallot
2 tablespoons sherry vinegar

generous pinch kosher salt
8 tablespoons extra virgin olive oil

Preparation

MAKE the vinaigrette:
PEEL the shallot and cut into small dice. Place in a small bowl with the vinegar and salt, and allow to macerate a bit. Whisk in the olive oil until combined and check for seasoning. Set aside while you assemble the salad.

PEEL the large tomatoes if the skin is tough, then core and cut into slices about ¼-inch thick. Halve the cherry tomatoes and small pear shaped tomatoes. Leave any very tiny tomatoes whole. Arrange the tomatoes attractively on either individual plates or a serving plate. Salt the tomatoes lightly.

TOSS the arugula leaves with some of the sherry vinaigrette, then arrange them attractively in the center, lifting to add a little height to the presentation.

SPRINKLE the blue cheese over and around the tomatoes, then drizzle with the remaining vinaigrette to taste. Finish with a generous grind of black pepper.

Serves 4

Sweet Waters

SweetWaters
AT VALLEY RIVER INN

1000 Valley River Way
Eugene, Oregon
541-743-1000
1-800-543-8266
www.valleyriverinn.com

Monday–Saturday
6:30 am–11:00 am
11:30 am–2:00 pm, 5:30 pm–9:30 pm
Sunday
7:30 am–2:00 pm, 5:30 pm–9:30 pm

Valley River Inn
Sweet Waters Restaurant
Michael Thieme, Executive Chef

No matter what table you have at the Sweet Waters Restaurant, you have a view of the Willamette River. This acclaimed restaurant is located in the Valley River Inn in Eugene. The menu offers Pan Pacific Northwest cuisine, featuring North American game, Pacific seafoods and locally gathered organic produce. Both the restaurant and the Executive Chef, Michael Thieme, have been featured in the pages of Bon Appetit, NW Palate and Simply Seafood.

Chef Thieme graduated from Le Cordon Rouge in Sausalito, California, in 1985. He traveled to Southeast Asia, Nepal, the Mediterranean and Britain, where he enhanced his culinary training with the regional influences he found there, incorporating unusual spice compositions and flavors. When he returned to California, Chef Thieme contributed his talents to several hotels and French restaurants in the bay area, including Christopher, La Terrace, Alexander's and Rive Gauche. He then moved to the Pacific Northwest, joining the Sweet Waters staff in 1988. At Sweet Waters, he indulges his passion for exotic and eclectic foods, bringing a fresh interpretation of the dining experience to the patrons of the restaurant.

Paul Martin, Sous Chef, was raised in south central Louisiana, and, not surprisingly, classic Creole dishes formed his first culinary influences. His career began in Austin, Texas, where he apprenticed at the acclaimed Jean Pierre's Upstairs, with San Francisco chef Janet Chekin, and also at the classic French bistro, Chez Nous. Paul's Oregon experiences include Timberline Lodge at Mt. Hood and Adam's Place in Eugene. Rounding out his resume, he spent a year at Las Canarias at La Mansion del Rio Hotel in San Antonio, Texas, where he worked under New York Chef Scott Cohen.

Sweet Waters Restaurants is part of the Valley River Inn, a resort-style hotel with meeting facilities, ballrooms and river view boardrooms. The resort offers tennis, golfing, bicycling, fishing, white water rafting and winery tours. Shopping is conveniently located next door, with 140 stores at the Valley River Center. The Sweet Waters Sunday Brunch, from 9 am to 2 pm, is one of Eugene's favorite brunch buffets, where you'll find salads, entrées, breakfast favorites, imported and domestic cheeses, fresh fruits, and desserts.

Friday and Saturday nights often feature some of the Northwest's best musical acts. When the weather allows, the festivities spill out onto the deck, in view of the magnificent Willamette River. Experience the warm days and clear nights from the comfort of this expansive, open-air veranda, and enjoy exquisite dining, accompanied by a glass of Oregon wine or a micro-brew.

CHIPOTLE PRAWNS
with Cilantro Linguini, Mango, Lime, and Tequila

Ingredients

- 1 pound cilantro linguini
- 2 tablespoons olive oil
- 1½ pounds large 16/20 prawns, peeled and de veined
- 1 tablespoons canned chipotle chilies, mixed with 4 ounces tomato juice
- 1 tablespoon minced garlic
- 1 small red pepper, cut into triangles
- 1 small yellow-pepper, cut into triangles
- ½ cup tequila
- 1 tomato, diced
- 1 mango, peeled, seeded, and diced
- 4 sprigs cilantro
- 1 lime

Preparation

BRING 4 quarts of lightly salted water to a boil. Drop pasta into water and cook until it is al denté or firm to the bite. Drain water and place pasta on the side.

IN A large sauté pan, heat oil over medium-high heat. Add prawns and sauté for 15 seconds. Add peppers and continue sautéing for about one minute more. Add garlic, stir once around, add chipotle chilies, stir, then add tequila. Cook off the alcohol and add tomatoes, stir once, taste and add salt if needed.

TO SERVE, place pasta on a large dish or platter. Arrange prawns around the pasta. Garnish with diced mango and sprigs of cilantro. Squeeze lime over the pasta and serve.

Serves 4

ROAST RACK OF VENISON
with Dijon Hazelnut Crust

Ingredients

3 racks of Venison - total of 4 pounds
cleaned with silverskin removed and rib
bones trimmed to 3" in length

1 cup hazelnuts - lightly toasted and
finely chopped

Dijon mustard

2 tablespoons fresh tarragon chopped
salt and pepper (optional)

3 ounces olive oil

Preparation

PREHEAT oven to 350 degrees.

SEAR racks in olive oil on high heat for 1 minute. Remove from pan and pat dry with paper towels.

RUB racks with tarragon and lightly season with salt and pepper. Spread a liberal amount of mustard on the loin with a spoon keeping the mustard off the rib bones.

PACK the hazelnuts on the loin pressing them into the meat with your hand.

PLACE racks in a roasting pan on a wire rack. Roast in pre-heated oven for 15 to 20 minutes. Internal temperature should reach 120 degrees for medium rare.

REMOVE from oven and let meat rest for fifteen minutes. Slice between Ribs and arrange on warmed plates.

Served with sautéed spring vegetables, mashed or roasted potatoes. Wild rice pilaf also works well.

Rack of lamb can be substituted for venison.

Suggested Beer - Brown or Amber Ale

Serves 6

PUMPKIN BISQUE
Laced with Coriander and Cardamom

Ingredients

2 *small sugar pumpkins*
1 *quart chicken stock*
1 *yellow onion, peeled and diced*
1 *head of garlic, roasted and peeled*
¼ *cup brandy*

½ *teaspoon ground coriander*
½ *teaspoon ground cardamom*
¼ *cup pumpkin seeds*
   salt & pepper

Preparation

CUT pumpkins in half and remove seeds. Rub the insides with olive oil & place on a sheet pan. Place cut side down and bake in a pre-heated oven at 350 ° for approximately 30 minutes. Let cool and scoop out the meat.

SAUTÉ onion over medium high heat, stir occasionally, until cooked through and lightly browned.

HEAT chicken stock in a medium saucepan, add onion, roasted pumpkin, brandy, coriander, cardamom and roasted garlic. Bring to a simmer and cook for about 30 minutes or until everything is cooked through and mushy.

PURÉE in a food processor or a hand blender. Taste and adjust seasonings. Keep on a low heat until ready to serve or cool and refrigerate.

SERVE in small pumpkin or squash bowls. Garnish with toasted pumpkin seeds.

Serves 4

WARM PEAR CUSTARD

Ingredients

16 ounces cream	1 vanilla bean
16 ounces milk	pinch nutmeg
6 eggs	6 whole pears (ripe)
⅔ cup sugar	white sugar

Preparation

PREHEAT oven to 325°. Cut the bottom of pears so they will stand, place on a sheet pan, roast in the oven for 30 to 40 minutes or until a skewer will easily go thru the pear. Remove from oven and let cool.

HEAT the milk, cream and vanilla bean together in a medium sauce pot just to the boiling point. Crack eggs into a mixing bowl, beat eggs until smooth. Do not over beat. Slowly pour hot cream into the eggs while stirring constantly. Strain.

BUTTER molds-fill them close to the top with the custard.

PLACE molds in a pan of hot water in the oven and bake test for doneness by inserting a small knife into the custard. If it comes out clean, it is done.

LET cool, to serve, peel the pear and cut into quarters. Remove core and slice thin. Arrange pear on top of the custard, sprinkle with about 1 tablespoon of sugar. Caramelize with a torch and serve.

Willie's
on 7th

Willie's *on 7th*

388 W. 7th
Eugene, Oregon
541-485-0601
www.willieson7th.com

Monday – Thursday
Dinner 5:00 pm – 9:00 pm
Friday – Saturday
5:00 pm – 10:00 pm

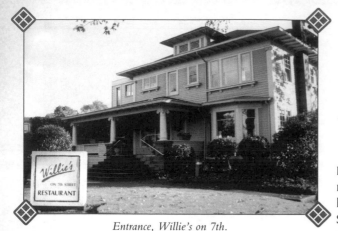
Entrance, Willie's on 7th.

Willie's on 7th
Walid Saleeby, Owner
Eric Melendez, Chef

Willie's On 7th in Eugene, is owned and operated by Walid Saleeby, a native of Beruit, Lebanon. The restaurant is located in a restored, spacious, turn-of-the-century home on the corner of 7th and Lawrence Street, two blocks from the center of town. The building was once part of the University of Oregon, and has been a restaurant for over 30 years, first as a restaurant named La Primavera. When Walid (Willie) and his partner took it over, they created Scampi's. In 1991, Scampi's closed, and Walid opened Willie's.

Willie's serves international cuisine, including dishes from Lebanon. Two daily specials are offered, prepared by Willie's chef, Eric Melendez. The menu is varied, including veal, Oregon lamb, fresh seafood, quail, duck, chicken, and pastas. The Specialties of the House are Broiled Northwest Lamb, rubbed with lemon pepper and drizzled with olive oil; and Roasted Half Duckling, glazed with apricot ginger sauce. Both are served with horseradish-mashed potatoes and vegetables.

Appetizers Include "Willie's Baba Ghannouj", a Lebanese classic with roasted eggplant, garlic and tahini dip, served with pita bread, and sautéed prawns, seasoned with Moroccan spices. Salads are multi-cultural, with Greek Salad and Fattoosh Salad, along with the perennial favorite, Caesar Salad. Pastas are unusual, too, from the Mose Pasta, with Cajun seasonings, to the Portobello Stuffed Ravioli, which has a jalepeno-infused vodka cream sauce on a bed of fire-roasted tomatoes.

Willie's has a good wine list with both local and international wines and beers, and a full service bar. The atmosphere is upscale casual.

NORTHWEST BROILED LAMB
with Lemon Pepper

This is a signature dish of Willies. NW lamb is a little less gamey than New Zealand or Australian lamb. Most people who maybe haven't liked lamb in the past usually like our lamb. This is an easy dish to do, and paired with our horseradish mashed potatoes it will make a great dinner.

Ingredients

- 15 bone in frenched lamb chops
- 3 tablespoons olive oil
- 3 tablespoons lemon pepper

Preparation

FIRST warm your grill. The cooking times given to you will be for medium done lamb. You can adjust cooking times for your desired doneness. Lay your lamb down on something flat, like a sheet pan. Coat the lamb with the olive oil. Then rub a generous amount of lemon pepper on each side of the lamb. Set the lamb on the grill and let sit for about 4 minutes. Then turn 45 degrees to get good cross marks, and let it cook for about another 2-4 minutes. Turn your lamb over and in about 4-6 minutes it will be done.

Note: sometimes its easier to find frenched rack of lamb. This will work fine. All you have to do is cut the chops buy cutting in between each bone.

Fattosh salad with Blackened Salmon

The fattosh salad is a wonderful Lebanese dish. With a dressing made from sumac, a tart mid eastern spice, this salad is very satisfying. Its a favorite of our owner to pair this salad with a blackened salmon fillet. Which turns this appetizing salad into a full meal.

Ingredients

5 8 ounces salmon fillets
1 cup blackening seasoning
2 tablespoons vegetable oil
1 medium tomato diced ¼ inch
1 cucumber diced ¼ inch
1 small sweet onion diced ⅛ inch

10 mint leaves chopped
3 loaves pita bread
2 heads romaine lettuce cleaned and chopped
1 cup sumac dressing

For the Sumac Dressing

5 cloves garlic minced fine
2 teaspoons salt
¾ cup lemon juice

⅓ cup sumac
⅓ cup water
¾ cup olive oil

Preparation

STICK the blackening seasoning on a plate. Dredge each salmon fillet in the seasoning. In a heavy duty skillet or sauté pan heat oil until it is very hot. Add salmon to the pan so that the side that the skin was on is facing up in the pan. Cook the salmon on that side until it is dark brown. Then turn them over and finish in a 400 degree oven, about 10 minutes in oven. While your salmon is cooking you can start putting together your salad. Take your pita and pull each one apart into two pieces. Place under a broiler until crisp and golden brown. Set aside to cool. In a big bowl add; tomatoes, cucumbers, onion, mint, and romaine. When the pita has cooled, break it up into bite size pieces and add it to the bowl. Add enough dressing to coat all the ingredients well, then toss together. To serve put salad on a plate and place a piece of blackend salmon on top.

For the Sumac Dressing

ADD all your ingredients except for the olive oil and mix well, then slowly whisk in the olive oil. This will hold for about two weeks.
Note: sumac is a dried spice that can be found in Mideastern markets.

Serves 5

Horseradish Mashed Potatoes

Ingredients

 5 russet potatoes peeled and quartered
¼ cup butter
½ cup heavy cream

1½ tablespoons horseradish
    salt & white pepper to taste

Preparation

IN A good sized stock pot, about 2 quarts, add potatoes and top off with water. Put on the stove to boil, and cook the potatoes until soft about 15-20 minutes. Strain potatoes and put them in a mixing bowl. Melt the butter with the heavy cream. Add that mixture and the horseradish to the potatoes and whip until smooth. Then add salt and pepper to taste.

Note: you can adjust the cream and the horseradish to taste if you like your potatoes creamier or spicier.

Logging near Knappa, Oregon - 1902.

Zane Gray fishing the North Umpqua

Steamboat Inn

42705 N. Umpqua Highway
Steamboat, Oregon
800-840-8825
541-498-2230
www.thesteamboatinn.com

Dinner hours begin:
Summer evenings at dusk
Winter evenings at 7:00 pm
By Reservation

Steamboat Inn

Jim & Sharon Van Loan, Proprietors
Patricia Lee, General Manager

The perfect retreat.

If you want to immerse yourself in nature and still have the luxury of comfortable accommodations and exceptional dining, Steamboat Inn is a perfect getaway. Located along the banks of the North Umpqua River, the inn has varied accommodations suited for many groups. Couples looking for a romantic weekend might like to check into one of the River Suites, featuring a fireplace, soaking tub and king-sized bed with a view of the river. A small family might enjoy one of the Hideaway Cottages located upstream in a nicely wooded and landscaped area. The spring wildflowers are a delight to view on the many hiking trails in the area, and draw photographers each spring to record their beauty.

Anyone interested in the fantastic steelhead fishing on the North Umpqua will find the Steamboat Inn a perfect retreat in the summer and fall. Fly fishers have revered this area of the river for more than a century, with the first fishing camps being established in the early 1920's. In the early 1930's Zane Grey moved his Oregon fishing trips from the Rogue River to the North Umpqua, and continued to camp there until his death in 1939.

The Steamboat Inn evolved from the camps and work of several couples that enjoyed hosting their friends and fishing clients on this famous river. One of the most important elements of the camps was the establishment of the Fisherman's Dinner. This tradition, started in the early 20th century, set the dinner hour at one half hour past sunset to allow all fishers the chance to fish the last light in the evening, which is usually the most productive for steelhead. Then, at dinner, they could share their fishing experiences and compare the flies and the techniques that they used.

Today, the Steamboat Inn still uses the huge table carved out of a sugar pine log in the 1930's for Clarence Gordon's North Umpqua Lodge. During the fishing season the Fisherman's Dinner is still the tradition, but with more emphasis on fresh local foods. Another tradition has become the Winemaker and Guest Chef Dinners that are popular on the weekends. Each dinner features a representative from a fine Oregon vineyard and usually a guest chef from a well-known Oregon restaurant. Since priority is given to overnight guests, be prepared to book reservations early.

Relax by the fireplace.

Basil-Parmesan Bread

Ingredients

3 large shallots, minced
2 cloves garlic, minced
2 tablespoons olive oil
2 cups warm water
2 tablespoons yeast

2 teaspoons salt
1¼ cups freshly grated Parmesan cheese
1½ cups minced fresh basil
3-4 cups flour

Preparation

SAUTÉ the shallots and garlic in the olive, just until they start to brown. Set aside to cool.

PROOF the yeast in the warm water for 10 minutes.

ADD the cooled shallot mixture along with the salt, cheese and minced basil to the proofed yeast.

GRADUALLY stir in the flour until you have a firm dough.

TURN out onto a lightly floured work surface and knead until smooth and elastic, adding flour as necessary to prevent the dough from sticking.

TRANSFER to a lightly oiled bowl and let rise until doubled in bulk.

WHEN risen, punch down and divide into three pieces and shape into rounds.

PLACE on a baking sheet dusted with cornmeal and let rise again until doubled.

PREHEAT oven to 400°.

SLIT the top of the loaves and sprinkle with kosher or sea salt.

BAKE for 25-40 minutes.

RACK OF LAMB

Ingredients

    2 1-1¼ pounds racks of lamb, trimmed

For the Marinade

    5 cloves garlic, minced
    2 teaspoons kosher salt
    1 teaspoon freshly ground black pepper
    3 4 inch sprigs fresh rosemary

    ½ cup olive oil
    ¼ cup red wine vinegar
    3 tablespoons soy sauce

Preparation

PLACE the trimmed lamb in a non reactive pan or bowl
STRIP the leaves from the rosemary sprigs. Discard the stems.
COMBINE the rosemary leaves and remaining marinade ingredients. Pour the marinade over the lamb and let set for 3 hours or overnight.

PREHEAT the oven to 400°

REMOVE the lamb from the marinade.
PLACE the racks on a baking sheet fat side up.
BAKE the racks 20-25 minutes for a rare doneness.
SLICE into individual chops and serve immediately

Serves 4-6

INDIVIDUAL PEAR TARTS

Ingredients

2 10 inch square sheets of puff pastry
4 ripe pears
2 tablespoons sugar
   (superfine if available)
   brown sugar

freshly grated nutmeg
ground cinnamon
vanilla extract
caramel sauce (recipe follows)
lightly sweetened whipped cream

Preparation

PREHEAT oven to 400° (375° convection)

LAY the puff pastry sheets out on a lightly floured work surface. Thoroughly prick the dough all over with a fork.

USING a 3" round cutter, cut 8 circles of puff pastry. Transfer to a parchment lined baking sheet. Invert a wire cooling rack onto the top of the puff pastry rounds.

BAKE the pastry for 10 minutes, just until it is light brown. Remove from the oven and remove the cooling rack from the top of the pastry rounds. Set aside. (This stage of baking the pastry can be done early in the day.)

WHEN ready to finish the dessert: Peel the pears and cut in half lengthwise. Remove the core.

CUT each pear half (lengthwise) into ⅛-¼" thick slices, without separating the slices.

TRANSFER the sliced pear half to a pastry round and press lightly to fan out the slices. Continue with the remaining pear halves.

DRIZZLE a small amount of vanilla over each pear. Top with a small amount of brown sugar, ground cinnamon and freshly grated nutmeg.

BAKE in the preheated oven 20 minutes, until the pears have softened.

SERVE warm with caramel sauce and lightly whipped cream;

For the Caramel Sauce

1½ cups sugar
½ cup water
1 cup heavy cream

COMBINE the sugar and water in a heavy-bottomed saucepan. Heat over medium heat until the sugar is dissolved, stirring occasionally.

WHEN the sugar is melted, raise the heat and continue to cook, without stirring, until the syrup turns a dark amber color. (Using a pastry brush dipped in water, occasionally wash down any sugar crystals that are on the sides of the pan.)

WHEN the sugar syrup is dark amber remove the pan from the heat.

CAREFULLY, and slowly, pour in the heavy cream, stirring until the cream is fully incorporated. Be very careful as the cool cream will spatter when added to the hot syrup.

IF THERE are any lumps, continue to stir with a whisk until the mixture is smooth. Strain into a bowl. Cover with a piece of plastic wrap or parchment to prevent a film from forming on the top of the caramel.

WHEN cool transfer to a storage container and refrigerate. The caramel will last several weeks in the refrigerator.

REHEAT before serving.

Makes 1 ½ cups.

Serves 8

Morrison's Rogue River Lodge

Opens May 1st each spring and closes in early – mid November each fall.
Dinner by reservation
Beginning at 7:00 pm or 7:30 pm, depending on time of year.

8500 Galice Road   541-476-3825
Merlin, Oregon   1-800-826-1963

Morrison's Rogue River Lodge

Morrison's Rogue River Lodge

B.A. & Michelle Hanten, Owners
Kurt Jacobsen, Chef

Built in the 1940's, Morrison's Rogue River Lodge has a rich history offering family hospitality and fine dining in a truly spectacular wilderness setting. Open from May 1st and closing in early to mid November, depending on the weather, the lodge offers a wonderful playground for those who wish to fish or raft on the Rogue River.

Originally built in 1946 by Lloyd Morrison to house his growing group of fishing clients, Lloyd did much of the construction himself, handpicking choice "birds-eye" pine logs from area forests. The fishing, the camaraderie, and the fine food helped Lloyd and Ruth quickly achieve an excellent reputation. Unfortunately, Ruth died in an untimely accident and Lloyd sold the lodge and started guiding on the Pacific, where he was lost at sea in 1956.

The lodge fell into disrepair for the next few years, but was purchased by B.A. and Elaine Hanten in 1964. Originally from South Dakota, the couple had been in the tourism industry in Yellowstone Park, and wanted to pursue the dream of owning their own fishing lodge. They took over the lodge just in time to see everything but the main lodge be swept away in the Big Flood of '64. It took several months to clean up and refurbish the lodge and build 3 new cottages in time for the next Fall Steelhead season. In 1986, an expansive outside deck overlooking the river was added to the front of the lodge, enabling Morrison's to open its doors to the dining public in the summer months. It's best to make reservations in advance, and the dinners are on a prix fixe menu, with choice of 2 entrees each evening.

As the years went by the Hantens and their family created their own unique charm for the lodge. Elaine's cooking expanded from good old-fashioned country cooking to gourmet cuisine, attracting many clients to return to the lodge every year. One of her inspired creations, the Orange Dinner Roll, is now a nightly staple. Several of her recipes have appeared in the RSVP section of Bon Appetit magazine. Regretfully, she passed away in 1996, but her fabulous recipes live on.

Although the lodge has grown in its reputation for fine dining and fine fishing, becoming an Orvis-endorsed lodge and adding raft trips, it still remains an intimate, unique experience, as close as you can get to the old "river lodge" personality for which the Rogue is famous.

Dining room, Rogue River Lodge.

Morrison's Rogue River Lodge, Merlin

CHILLED CUCUMBER SOUP
Appetizer

This refreshing summer soup is one of Morrison's signature dishes. It is hands down the most often requested dish we serve in the summer. A great beginning to any summer meal. The receipe is simple and can be made ahead of time.

Ingredients

Blend well in blender or food processor

2 cups chicken stock	½ cup chopped onion
3 cucumbers, peeled & seeded	1 small clove garlic

Transfer to large container and whisk in

2 cups sour cream	1 teaspoon salt
3 tablespoons. rice vinegar	½ teaspoon white pepper

Preparation

CHILL well.
SERVE in chilled bowls.

GARNISH in each bowl with 1 teaspoon tomato salsa by gently spooning the salsa in the middle of the bowl.

Serves 8 (⅔ cup servings)

STUFFED FIGS
Appetizer

With fig trees on the Lodge property, we had long searched for ways to serve figs. This appetizer is outstanding. We now wish we had fresh figs year around.

Ingredients

Wash
>   12 *fresh figs*

Pat dry and cut the stem end off. With your thumb make a hole in the center of the fig to make a cup.

Chop
>   1 *teaspoon fresh rosemary*

In a mixing bow mix with:
>   1 *cup fresh goat cheese*

FILL figs with cheese mixture.
CUT thinly sliced prosciutto into strips long enough to wrap around the outside of each fig leaving the top open. Wrap figs with prosciutto, secure by tucking the end around the wrapped portion. Place figs on a cookie sheet. Heat at 325° for approximately 5 minutes, just to warm through.
ON A plate, garnish with endive leaves, or wild greens.

Serve 3 or 4

SPINACH SALAD
with Pear-Apple Chutney Dressing

Ingredients

  2 *bunches spinach*
½ *cup radishes*
⅓ *cup green onions*
  5 *slices bacon*
½ *cup water chestnuts*
½ *cup cheddar cheese*

For the Dressing

  1 *cup canola oil*
½ *cup Morrison's Pear-Apple Chutney*
¼ *cup red wine vinegar*
  1 *small clove garlic*
  1 *tablespoon onion*
  1 *tablespoon Dijon mustard*
  1 *tablespoon sugar*
     dash salt & pepper

Preparation

CUT 5 slices bacon into ¼ inch pieces. Cook until crispy, drain, set aside to cool.

WASH 2 bunches of spinach. Cut the spinach into 1½ inch slices and spin dry.

SLICE ½ cup radishes
        ⅓ cup green onions
IN A large salad bowl toss together spinach, radishes, onions, bacon and
        ½ cup of drained water chestnuts
        ½ cup of grated cheddar cheese

TOSS salad with enough Pear-Apple Chutney dressing to gently dress salad. Garnish with a fresh tomato wedge.

For the Pear-Apple Chutney Dressing

BLEND ingredients in a blender, on medium, until almost smooth.
Makes about 1½ cups of dressing. Dressing can be stored in a closed container the refrigerator for up to 2 weeks.

Serves 6-8

BAKED POTATOES N' CREAM

The idea for this recipe originally came from James Beard, we have our own version that is just a little different but just as wonderful. Not for anyone on a diet.

Ingredients

4 large baked potatoes	salt & pepper
1 cube butter	½ cup Swiss cheese
1⅓ cup heavy cream	

Preparation

BAKE at 400° 4 large potatoes until just done.

CUT each potato in half the long way and scoop out the inside into a well greased 2 quart baking dish. When about ½ full sprinkle salt and pepper to taste and dot with ½ cube of butter

POUR over all 2/3 cup heavy cream

SCOOP out remaining potatoes and repeat with ½ cube of butter and 2/3 cup heavy cream

SPRINKLE ½ cup Swiss cheese over the top and bake for 30 minutes at 350°. Remove from oven and let stand for 10 minutes before serving.

Serves 8

BROCCOLI WITH BROWNED BUTTER
AND TOASTED ALMONDS

Ingredients

  2 *bunches of broccoli*
½ *cup butter*
½ *cup sliced almonds*

Preparation

WASH and trim 2 bunches of broccoli
PREPARE to steam in vegetable steamer. A saucepan with a steaming basket is fine. Place broccoli in steam tray and fill bottom of steamer with water. Set aside until ready to cook.

IN A saucepan add:
     ½ cup butter
     ½ cup sliced almonds
HEAT over medium heat until butter starts to brown. Almonds should get nice and toasted. Be careful not to burn. This can be done ahead of time and then heated up when ready to serve.

BRING water in steamer to a boil. Steam broccoli for 3-5 minutes or to desired doneness, should be bright green in color. Transfer to a serving dish and spoon over browned butter and almonds. Serve immediately.

Serves 8–12

Roast Duck Breast
with Plum Sauce

This dish is served often in the fall fishing season accompanied by a wild rice pilaf and baked winter squash.

Ingredients

8   *5-6 ounce duck breasts*
1   *tablespoon canola oil*

For Seasoning Rub

1   *teaspoon fennel seed*
3   *teaspoon anise seed*
½   *teaspoon white pepper*
1   *teaspoon rosemary leaf*
½   *teaspoon sage*
1   *teaspoon thyme leaf*
2   *teaspoon paprika*
2   *teaspoon salt*
1   *tablespoon cinnamon*

For Plum Sauce

2   *tablespoons butter*
6   *tablespoons sugar*
⅔   *cup apple cider vinegar*
1   *quart plum juice from fresh plums (or canned plums in juice pitted and puréed)*
1   *pint plum jelly (or red currant jelly)*
2   *inch piece of fresh ginger*
1   *tablespoon cornstarch*
¼   *cup water*

Preparation

TRIM excess fat from 8 duck breasts leaving skin on. Add to a skillet 1 tablespoon canola oil

SEAR breasts in a hot skillet with skin side down until skin starts to crisp, about 5 minutes, do not turn breasts over. Remove from skillet to a cooling rack and allow to drain. After breasts are cooled, rub entire breast with seasoning rub. Place in a baking pan on a rack with skin side up. Cook at 350° uncovered for 20 - 25 minutes.

SERVE duck breasts immediately from the oven with Plum Sauce spooned over each breast.

For Seasoning Rub
MIX together ingredients.

For the Plum Sauce
IN A heavy bottom 2½-quart saucepan add:
      2 tablespoons butter
      6 tablespoons sugar

BRING to a boil, stirring often until caramelized, approximately 5 minutes. Remove from heat. Add:

⅔ cup apple cider vinegar

1 quart plum juice

1 pint plum jelly (or red currant jelly)

2-inch piece of fresh ginger cut into slices

RETURN to heat and bring to a boil stirring occasionally. Once it comes to a boil reduce to a simmer and allow to reduce by ⅓, approximately 15 - 20 minutes.

THICKEN sauce with a mixture of:

1 tablespoon cornstarch

¼ cup cold water

WHISK into sauce, bring to a slow boil and cook 1 minute. You may add more cornstarch mixture if needed to bring to desired thickness. Remove from heat, cool slightly and pour through a sieve. Serve generously over duck breasts.

Wine Recommendations: A hearty Gewurtztraminer is a great accompaniment to this dish. Or if you prefer a red, we suggest a elegant Pinot Noir, such as a Domaine Drouhin.

Serves 8

Outdoor dining.

Hunting camp.

Jacksonville Inn

175 E. California St.
Jacksonville, Oregon
541-899-1900
1-800-321-9344
www.jacksonvilleinn.com

Breakfast 7:30 – 10:30 am, daily
Lunch 11:30 am- 2:00 pm Tuesday-Saturday
Sunday Brunch 10:00 am – 2:00 pm
Dinner - Monday-Saturday
5:00 – 10:00 pm;
Sunday 5:00 - 9:00 pm

Cottage garden.

Jacksonville Inn
Jerry & Linda Evans, Owners

Take a moment to leave Interstate 5 near Medford, and you will be rewarded with the inviting little town of Jacksonville. Founded in 1852, Jacksonville has preserved much of its western heritage with more than 80 pioneering buildings sporting historical markers. The first discovery of gold in the Pacific Northwest occurred here. The main street, which houses the Jacksonville Inn, is picturesque with its clapboard fronts and sidewalks.

Take time to walk around and enjoy the friendly ambience of the town. Then, check in at the Jacksonville Inn for a comfortable evening in one of their eight hotel rooms or one of the four honeymoon cottages nearby. Each room is furnished with authentic western antiques and includes a private bath. Within walking distance of the Inn is the Britt Music and Arts Festival. Running from early June through the first weekend in September, the town plays host to international musicians who present superb concerts nightly in the beautiful Britt Gardens.

Dining at the Inn is a fun experience. With over 1500 fine wines from which to select, it is no wonder that the establishment has won the coveted Wine Spectator "Best of Award of Excellence". Dinner can be enjoyed in the main dining room, downstairs in the Bistro Lounge, or outside in a beautiful garden setting in the patio. The downstairs dining room is enhanced with the specks of gold that are still visible in the mortar binding together the blocks of locally mined sandstone that form the walls.

There is something for everyone on the dinner menu, from tantalizing steaks and filets to fresh wild Pacific Rim Salmon and Dungeness Crab Legs. You can also find wild game on the menu. A favorite is the Northern Velvet Venison, marinated in olive oil, garlic, Dijon mustard and rosemary, then coated with a breadcrumb hazelnut crust and served with an apple cider sauce. Another specialty is the Pancetta Wrapped Bison Steak with Truffle Polenta and Green Peppercorn Demi Glace.

Outdoor dining area.

 Wine Spectator Award

JACKSONVILLE INN CHICKEN

Ingredients

6 5 ounce skinless boneless chicken
   breasts
2 cups coarsely chopped hazelnuts

1 cup fine cracker meal
2 beaten eggs
2 cups peanut oil

For the Sauce

3 cups Martinellis sparkling cider
½ cup white wine vinegar
½ cup cassis liquor
½ cup brandy

½ cup chicken stock
1½ cup heavy cream
   Salt and pepper

For the Filling

1 green apple peeled and cored and finely diced
1 celery rib finely diced
½ small onion finely diced
2 minced garlic cloves
1 minced shallot
4 tablespoons butter

2 tablespoons brandy
1 tablespoon dried sage
¼ teaspoon allspice
Salt and freshly ground pepper
6 ounces cream cheese

Preparation

PREPARE the first five ingredients, heat a large sauté pan to medium and melt four tablespoons butter. Add the apple, celery, onion, shallot, and garlic. Cook slowly, stirring often, until translucent. Add brandy, sage, and allspice. Remove from heat and stir in cream cheese until completely incorporated and soft. Season with salt and pepper and spread on a cookie sheet. Refrigerate until cold.

To Assemble

COMPLETELY flatten the chicken breasts between two sheets of waxed paper. Place ⅙ of filling mixture on center of flattened chicken breast. Tuck sides in over the filling and roll up "burrito" style. When all breasts are stuffed and rolled, beat 2 eggs in a small mixing bowl. Combine hazelnuts and cracker meal in another small bowl. Dip chicken breasts in egg, then roll in hazelnut mixture, patting firmly so the hazelnuts adhere well. Refrigerate while heating peanut oil in a heavy –bottomed pan. When oil is hot, brown chicken breasts. Place on cookie sheet and bake 25-30 minutes at 350° until a thermometer registers 160 internal degrees. Spoon sauce on plate. Slice chicken breast into 5-6 slices and fan on plate over the sauce.

Serves 6

Eola Hills Chardonnay Mystery Block 2001 (Wine Spectator 90 points)
Kim Crawford Savvignon Blanc 2003 (Wine Spectator 90 points)

Seared Alaskan Halibut
with Clams, Mussels, and Shrimp
in a Saffron Red Pepper Sauce, Served with Ratatouille

Ingredients

4 5 ounce pieces Alaskan halibut
20 Manila clams, cleaned
20 black mussels, cleaned and de bearded

8 large shrimp
(peeled and de veined – tail on)

For the Ratatouille

1 small eggplant peeled and cut into a large disc
1 small zucchini peeled and cut into a large disc
1 small red onion peeled and cut into a large disc
1 small red pepper peeled and cut into a large disc

1 small yellow pepper peeled and cut into a large disc
3 cups cleaned spinach
1 tablespoon chopped garlic
olive oil as needed
salt and pepper

For the Sauce

3 tablespoons olive oil
1 medium onion coarsely chopped
3 cloves garlic chopped
2 large red bell peppers chopped
1 leek (white part only) chopped
1 15 ounces can diced tomatoes

1 cup white wine
1 cup clam juice
1 bay leaf
1 large pinch saffron threads
1 pinch red chili flakes

Preparation

For the Sauce

HEAT a medium saucepan, add olive oil and then the onion, garlic, red bell pepper and leek. Cook, stirring often until the vegetables are translucent. Add the rest of the ingredients and simmer for 20 minutes. Purée in batches in a blender and strain sauce through a medium sieve. Season with salt and pepper and keep warm.

For the Ratatouille

CUT each vegetable into a uniform dice. Do not mix vegetables until after they are cooked as each has a different cooking time.
FILM a heavy-bottomed large sauté pan with olive oil and heat to high. Sauté each vegetable until cooked through and remove to a mixing bowl. When the first five ingredients are cooked, sauté spinach and garlic. Mix all ingredients together, season with salt and pepper and keep warm.

To Assemble

HEAT a heavy-bottomed large sauté pan to medium-high. Add olive oil and then halibut. Cook until halibut is browned on one side (about 4-5 minutes). Turn halibut over and add shellfish and about 8 ounces of reserved saffron sauce. Bring to a simmer. Cover and cook another 5 minutes, or until shellfish has opened and halibut is cooked through.

PLACE each halibut filet in a deep pasta bowl and divide shellfish and shrimp among the four bowls. Spoon the sauce around each fish (about 4-6 ounces each portion). Top the fish with ratatouille and sprinkle with chopped parsley.

Wine Suggestion: Hamacher Pinot Noir 2000, Carlton, Oregon, Robert Parker 92 points
Hamacher Chardonnay 2000, Carlton, Oregon, Robert Parker 89 points

Serves 4

Room 1 at the Jacksonville Inn.

Cottage 12 at the Jacksonville Inn.

Pear/Walnut Salad

Ingredients

For the Dressing
½ apple – peeled, cored, and cut into chunks
1 small shallot – minced
1 tablespoon honey
1 tablespoon sugar
¾ cup walnut oil
¾ cup cider vinegar
salt and fresh ground pepper

For the Seasoned Walnuts
1 cup walnut halves
1 egg white
½ teaspoon salt
1 tablespoon sugar
¼ teaspoon (or to taste) cayenne

For the Pears
3 pears peeled, cut into quarters, and cored
½ cup red wine
½ cup water
¼ cup sugar
1 bay leaf
1 cinnamon stick
peel from ½ of a lemon

For the Salad
1 small package Spring Mix lettuce
1 cup red seedless grapes
½ cup crumbled bleu cheese

Preparation

For the Dressing
PLACE the apple and shallot in a food processor and pulse until smooth. With the motor running, add the honey, sugar, and vinegar. Slowly add the walnut oil. Season to taste with salt and pepper. Use immediately or refrigerate in a tightly closed jar. Shake before using.

For the Pears
PREPARE pears; combine all of the other ingredients in a small saucepan. Place pears in wine mixture. Add more wine or water if necessary to cover pears. Bring to a simmer and cook for five minutes. Remove from heat. Cool and refrigerate until cold.

For the Seasoned Walnuts
PLACE egg whites in a small mixing bowl. Add the salt, sugar and cayenne. Whisk until foamy. Add walnuts and toss to coat well. Spread on a Teflon baking sheet and toast in a 325° oven stirring often, until toasted. Cool before using.

To Assemble Salad

PLACE lettuce and grapes in a mixing bowl and toss with the apple-walnut vinaigrette. Divide salad and grapes onto six plates. Divide the poached pears and sprinkle the salads with the seasoned walnuts and crumbled bleu cheese.

Wine Suggestion: St. Innocent Pinot Gris, Shea Vineyard 2000, Salem, OR; Robert Parker 89 points
Luna Pinot Grigio, Napa, CA 2001; Steven Tanzer 90-92 points

Serves 6

COCONUT, LEMON GRASS AND BUTTERNUT SQUASH
with Sticky Rice and Thai Herbs Soup

Ingredients:

1 pound turnips	12 cans coconut milk
½ pound parsnips	4½ roasted butternut squash
½ pound carrots	1½ tablespoons curry power
2½ pounds lemon grass	1 tablespoon ground fennel
1¾ pounds yellow onions	1 tablespoon ground cinnamon
1 pound celery	1 tablespoon ground corriander
⅓ pound ginger	½ tablespoon ground star anise
1 tablespoon red curry	1½ cups fish sauce
5 Kefir lime leaves	

Preparation

Roast seedless Butternut Squash in 350° oven for about 1½ hours or until soft. Cool and skin – reserve. Sauté mire-poix until tender, then add red curry paste and sauté for additional five minutes. Add squash, coconut milk, and Kefir lime – whisk together. Bring to a simmer and cook for 30 minutes. Add fish sauce and spices. Purée and strain through a large hole strainer. Garnish with 2 tablespoons. Sticky calrose rice and Thai herbs (cilantro, mint, and basil – equal portions of each).

Serves 15

Wine Suggestion: Roger Lassarat Vergisson White Burgandy 2002 Macon, France.
Loosen Brothers "DRL" Reisling 2002, Bernkastel/Mosel, Germany.

CHAR BROILED ELK FILET
with Butternut Squash and Foie Gras

Ingredients

16 slices sourdough bread without crust or heels, air-dried for 4 hours   butternut squash

For the Custard

2 quarts heavy whipping cream
½ pound brown butter
   zest of 2 lemons, 1 orange
1 cup roasted hazelnuts
½ large butternut squash roasted

1¼ cup egg yolks
1 teaspoon salt
1 teaspoon pepper
4 teaspoons chopped tarragon
1½ teaspoons fresh ground nutmeg

For the Elk

6 6 ounce portions
1 teaspoon sate paste
2 tablespoons coriander
1 tablespoon curry
1 tablespoon fennel

For the Demi–Glace

1 teaspoon sate paste
2 tablespoons coriander
1 tablespoon curry
1 tablespoon fennel

1 tablespoon kosher salt
1 tablespoon cracked pepper
1 tablespoon fresh chopped thyme
3 tablespoons extra virgin olive oil

Preparation

ROAST seeded butternut squash with ¼ pound butter in 350° oven 1¼ hours or until soft. Cool and skin. Slice bread and air dry. Mix the custard. Soak bread and line in terrene mold. Add squash through middle of mold, then add more soaked break on top. Cover and cook for 30 minutes in 350° oven.

SEAR elk to desired temperature, then sear foie gras on high heat – add demi-glace to foie gras. Slice bread pudding and place in center of plate. Place elk on top and sauce around the main dish.

Note: Sate paste is available in most Asian grocery stores.

Wine Suggestion:
Valley View Meritage 1999, Jacksonville, OR
Abacela Syrah 2001, Roseburg, OR

Serves 6

Chateaulin Restaurant Francais

Chateaulin

52 E. Main St. Rm. 19
Ashland, Oregon
541-482-2264
www.chateaulin.com

Wednesday–Sunday 5:30 pm

Chateaulin
Restaurant Francais
David Taub, Chef and Co-Owner
Jason Doss, Co-Owner and Manager

1914 Rodeo

The friendly little town of Ashland is a Mecca for those who love theatre and fine dining. Ashland is the home of the Oregon Shakespeare Festival, the nation's oldest and largest theatre in rotating repertory. With three theatres, the company presents eleven plays – five by Shakespeare and six by classic and contemporary playwrights – in its season from mid-February to early November.

Nestled very close to the theatre complex is Chateaulin Restaurant Francais, a romantic storefront café that has been at the top of the list of Oregon's best restaurants since its establishment in 1973.

David Taub, was hired as the Chef's Assistant in the restaurant's opening year. He left shortly after this to pursue his degree at the Culinary Institute of America in Hyde Park, NY. After graduating in 1977, he returned to become Chef and co-owner of Chateaulin.

David keeps the menu fresh with seasonal changes based on the network of local growers and ranchers that he has encouraged in the Pacific Northwest. Although he predominantly uses local ingredients, David's philosophy also includes searching for prime ingredients from far-reaching areas of the world, such as New Zealand venison and Hawaiian swordfish. His European travels and his education at the Culinary Institute have instilled in him a love of the French cooking techniques.

One can see this influence in the superb French Onion Soup baked with Emmenthal Swiss cheese that is a house standard. Or, try the Pate Maison, a country-style loaf of veal, pork, pistachio nut and Cognac. The entrees will delight the palate, ranging from a vegetarian Crepes a la Florentine to a classic French duck breast: Magret de Canard au Gingembre, a Muscovy duck breast served with a sherry, soy, and ginger glaze and served with sautéed baby bok choy.

The Chateaulin dining experience is heightened by the fact that, if you happened to like a particular wine, you can stroll next door to the Chateaulin Wine Shop that is run by co-owner and manager, Jason Doss. Jason loves to share wine stories with his many repeat customers, and is an enthusiastic promoter of the lovely Ashland area.

SHRIMP CAKES
with Ginger Sesame Slaw and Meyer Lemon Creme Fraiche
Appetizer

When fresh crab season ended one spring, we got the idea to try some Oregon bay shrimp cakes. It has been a well received first course ever since.

Ingredients

1	pound bay shrimp meat, fresh – drained of excess liquid	1	teaspoon chili flakes
1	egg	1	cup mayonnaise
3	tablespoons Dijon mustard	1	tablespoon chopped parsley
1	tablespoon dried mustard	2	green onions, chopped
1	teaspoon ground black pepper	3	cups (plus) panko bread crumbs (Japanese style bread crumbs)

For the Ginger Sesame Slaw

1	cup fresh ginger, peeled	1	cup mayonnaise
1	tablespoon rice vinegar	1	cup sour cream
1	cup water	1	teaspoon sugar
1	head green cabbage, cored and shredded	2	tablespoon black sesame seeds
1	head red cabbage, cored and shredded		salt and fresh ground black pepper to taste

For the Meyer Lemon Creme Fraiche

1	cup creme fraiche	1	tablespoon finely chopped chives
2	large meyer lemons (can substitute with 2 limes and one regular lemon)	1	tablespoon finely chopped Italian parsley

Preparation

DIVIDE the bay shrimp, leaving half whole and coarsely chopping the remainder.

IN A large stainless steel bowl, mix together the egg, Dijon mustard, dried mustard, black pepper, chili flakes, mayonnaise, parsley and green onions. Add all the shrimp. Mix until well combined. Add the panko bread crumbs. Form into 16 patties and store on a bed of additional panko bread crumbs until ready to cook.

IN AN ovenproof sauté pan, heat clarified butter over medium heat. Once the pan is hot, add the shrimp cakes and cook until the one side is browned. Turn the cakes over and put the pan into a 350 degree oven for 10 minutes or until the other side is browned and the cakes are heated through. Serve on ginger sesame slaw (recipe below) with meyer lemon crème fraiche sauce (recipe below) on the side. Garnish with a sprinkle of black sesame seeds and lemon wedges.

For the Ginger Sesame Slaw

IN A blender combine ginger, rice vinegar and water and blend until smooth. If necessary, add a few more drops of water to facilitate blending.

IN A large stainless steel bowl, combine remaining ingredients and ginger paste. Season with salt and pepper. Keep chilled until ready to use.

For the Meyer Lemon Creme Fraiche

FINELY chop the zest of both lemons. Juice the lemons and strain into a small sauce pot. Reduce by 1. Let cool.

COMBINE cooled juice, zest, herbs and creme fraiche. Keep cold until ready to use.

Serves 6–8

Roast Rack of Lamb
with Creamy Garlic White Beans and Rosemary Zinfandel Reduction

This dish has become a mainstay at Chateaulin using fresh Willamette Valley lamb. We garnish it with wilted fresh chard.

Ingredients

2 sides rack of lamb, frenched and trimmed of most of the fat - preferably fresh and domestic

1 cup cannellini beans (dried) - soaked overnight in cold water

1 sprig fresh rosemary

3 cloves garlic - finely chopped

3 sprigs fresh parsley

1 cup shallots - chopped

1 bay leaf

1 cup heavy cream
1 750 ml bottle Zinfandel wine
2 quarts brown lamb stock
1 sprig fresh thyme

1 teaspoon black peppercorn
   salt and fresh ground black pepper to
   taste
2 tablespoons extra virgin olive oil

For the Marinade

2 tablespoon extra virgin olive oil
3 cloves garlic - finely chopped
1 sprig fresh rosemary - finely chopped

Preparation

TO MARINATE the lamb. Rub the racks with the olive oil then toss with the garlic and rosemary. Marinate for at least 2 hours.

For the Creamy Garlic White Beans

DRAIN the soaked cannellini beans, put in a heavy bottomed saucepan and cover with cold water. Salt the water lightly and bring to a boil. Turn the heat down to a simmer and cook until the beans are tender. Drain, returning 1 cup of the cooking liquid to the pan with the beans. Add the cream and 1 tablespoon of finely chopped thyme, ½ the chopped garlic and simmer until lightly thick. Remove from heat and keep warm.

For the Sauce

IN A large saucepan, combine the wine, remaining garlic and thyme, rosemary, parsley, shallot, bay leaf and peppercorns. Reduce liquid to 1 cup. Add the brown lamb stock and reduce again until lightly thick. Strain sauce and keep warm.

For the Lamb

SEASON the marinated lamb racks generously with salt and pepper. In an oven proof sauté pan, heat the 2 tablespoons of olive oil over moderate heat. Add the lamb racks and brown on both sides. Pour off the excess fat after browning, and place in an 400° oven roasting to medium rare turning once (about 10 minutes per side).
REMOVE the lamb and let the meat rest at least 5 minutes. Carve the rack into individual chops and plate them leaning the chops on the Creamy Garlic White Beans surrounded by the sauce.

Serves 4

Chocolate Raspberry Roulade

The roulade has been a signature dessert at Chateaulin for years. It combines a lightness with enough richness to be a perennial favorite of our customers.

Ingredients

Cake
6 eggs, separated
2 tablespoon espresso
1 teaspoon vanilla
6 ounces semi sweet chocolate, melted
3 cup sugar
butter and flour for the pan

Sauce
raspberry sauce

Filling
1 pint heavy cream
1 cup powdered sugar
1 tablespoon Chambord liquor

Ganache
6 ounces semi sweet chocolate, chopped
5 ounces heavy cream

Preparation

BUTTER and flour one sheet pan (12"x18"x1"). Line the sheet pan with parchment paper leaving an overhang on one edge, and butter the paper. Preheat oven to 400 degrees.

IN A large stainless steel bowl, whisk together the egg yolks, espresso and vanilla. Add the melted chocolate and mix well.

IN A large mixer, beat the egg whites on high until soft peaks form. Slowly add the 3 cup of sugar and continue beating until stiff peaks form. Whisk 1 cup of the egg whites into the chocolate mixture until well blended. Fold in the remaining egg whites.

SPREAD the cake batter evenly into the buttered pan. Bake for 13 minutes, open the oven door for 2 seconds, turn the heat down to 350° and bake an additional 6 minutes. Take the cake out of the oven. Run a knife along the edges of the pan, and pull the cake out of the pan using the overhanging parchment paper as a handle. Let the cake sit on a flat surface until cool to the touch.

IN A chilled mixer bowl, whip the heavy cream until soft peaks form, then add the powdered sugar and Chambord liquor. Continue beating until stiff peaks form. Turn the cake lengthwise and spread the cream onto 3 of the sides leaving the edge furthest away uncovered, and roll the cake as you would a jelly roll.

TO MAKE the ganache, bring the cream to a boil, remove from heat and pour over the chopped chocolate. Whisk together until smooth.

POUR the warm ganache over the rolled cake and place on a platter.

REFRIGERATE for at least 4 hours before serving.

SERVE with raspberry sauce.

Serves 10

Shakespeare Festival — Ashland.

Grave Creek covered bridge

Monet

36 S. 2nd St.
Ashland, Oregon
541-482-1339
www.mind.net/monet

Tuesday–Sunday
5:30 pm–8:30 pm
Closed in January
Closed Sunday and Monday
during off-season

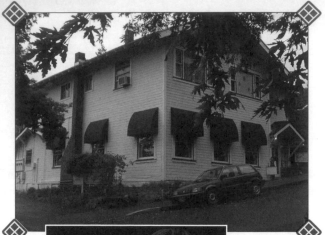

Monet
Pierre & Dale Verger, Owners
Pierre Verger, Chef

Chef Pierre Verger and his wife, Dale, own and operate Monet Restaurant and Garden, which they opened in the fall of 1991. Monet is named for the famous French impressionist, Claude Monet, and the interior of the restaurant is decorated with colors from the artist's palette. Pale pinks and greens are found throughout, with soft peach accents highlighting the front windows. The walls are covered with French batting and have replicas of Monet's oil paintings. Fresh flowers, floral tablecloths, and stylish, comfortable chairs set off each table, and the soft tones of classical music complete the intimately elegant ambiance. The garden, offering outside dining from mid-June to September, includes plants similar to those featured in Monet's garden. The overall effect is one of tranquility and romance, encouraging diners to take time to unwind and enjoy the Monet dining experience.

Dale and Pierre Verger

With a setting so carefully planned, it's no surprise the food is prepared and presented with utmost care. The authentic French cuisine, prepared by Chef Pierre, is a visual and culinary delight, with fresh herbs and flowers from the garden, in season. Described as traditional French country with a light touch, Chef Pierre's talents are authentic. He began his training in his hometown of Tain-l'Hermitage in the Rhone Valley in France, and continued at the renowned Plaza Athenee Hotel in Paris. This is Pierre's fourth restaurant, having operated two restaurants in the California bay area, L'Hermitage and St. Moritz, and one on Long Island, Pierre's Chalet.

Monet hosts several special events throughout the year, including Winemaker Dinners, and as it is located within blocks of the theater, the restaurant is also a favorite spot for the theater crowd.

Dining room, Monet.

Monet, Ashland

158

SAUMON FUMÉ À LA MOUSSE D'AVOCAT
Appetizer

This is a beautiful appetizer that our customers look forward to finding on our summer menu. It is a recipe that Chef Pierre brought back from France in 1995 when he visited for several weeks. This recipe goes well with a Sancerre or a glass of champagne.

Ingredients

- 3 avocados
- 3 lemons
  fresh ground pepper, sea salt, and parsley for decoration
- 7 tablespoons olive oil or hazelnut oil
- 4 slices of smoked salmon (cold smoked salmon, like lox)
- 3 garlic cloves
- 5 ounces butter
  salt, pepper

Preparation

PEEL the avocados and then cut them in pieces. Juice the three lemons. Peel the garlic and chop it finely.

IN THE food processor, blend the avocado and the butter. While still blending, pour in the olive oil and add salt and pepper to taste. Add in half of the lemon juice and continue blending.

Presentation

PUT one tablespoon of avocado mousse on the end of each slice of smoked salmon. Roll each one and serve on a vinaigrette of the reserved lemon juice and olive oil. Sprinkle with freshly ground pepper, sea salt and decorate with sprigs of parsley.

Serves 4

MIGNON DE PORC AU GINGEMBRE

One of our popular entrees at Monet. Pork is always popular with a fruit of some kind. The fresh raspberries and ginger in the sauce make your palate zing. If you prefer, this recipe could be made with veal or lamb as well. Serve with a white St Joseph from Chef Pierre's home region of the Rhone Valley.

Ingredients

1 *filet mignon of pork*
1 *piece of fresh ginger root*
7 *tablespoons of raspberry vinegar*
½ *cup fresh or frozen raspberries*
   butter as needed

3 *shallots*
4 *tablespoons of veal stock*
   (or equivalent in bouillon cube)
   salt, pepper

Preparation

PEEL the pork tenderloin. Cut it in small slices of about 1 inch in thickness. Chop the shallots and cut the ginger in a fine julienne. Blanche the ginger twice.
SAUTÉ the pork lightly in oil and butter until cooked to your taste. Salt and pepper.
SET the pork aside and keep warm.
IN ANOTHER saucepan, boil water to dissolve the bouillon cube. If you are using veal stock, the water is not needed.
REMOVE the fat from the pan in which you cooked the pork. Sauté the shallots.
DEGLAZE the pan with the raspberry vinegar.
ADD the veal stock and reduce the mixture for a few minutes. Add some of the ginger. Whip some butter, cut in little pieces, into the sauce to finish.
PLACE the pork on a serving dish and cover it lightly with the sauce.
SPRINKLE with the rest of the ginger.

Serve accompanied by your favorite vegetables.

Serves 4

Chèvre Chaud Rôti Aux Amandes

This salad is a great starter or perfect as a light supper on a hot night. The warm goat cheese makes a perfect contrast to the cool salad. Serve with a Sauvignon Blanc.

Ingredients

1   log goat cheese – form 4 round shapes
    bread crumbs
    flour
2   ounces chopped almonds
    Salad mix for 4 servings
2   teaspoons mustard
7   tablespoons crème fraiche

1   bunch of chives - some chopped and
    several left long for decoration
    vinegar, olive oil
1   egg
2   tablespoon butter
    salt, pepper

Preparation

IN A shallow dish, mix the bread crumbs and the chopped almonds. Make sure your mixture is predominately bread crumbs and not too much almonds, or the mixture will not hold together.

BREAK the egg into another shallow dish. Salt and pepper to taste. Add a drop of olive oil and beat the mixture like an omelette. Put the flour in a third shallow dish.

PASS each goat cheese first in flour, then in egg, and last in the bread crumb/almond mixture. PUT them aside.

CLEAN and wash the salad greens. Dry them and set aside.

PREPARE the vinaigrette with salt, pepper, vinegar, mustard, crème fraiche and chopped chives.

JUST AS you are ready to serve the salad tossed with the vinaigrette, cook the goat cheese rounds in a frying pan that contains 3 tablespoons butter. Turn the cheese rounds from time to time and serve them hot on the cool salad.

Serves 4

CANARD AU MIEL DE LAVANDE ET AU CITRON

This entrée is very impressive. The lavender honey has more perfume than sugar. Some people say you judge a restaurant by the way the duck is prepared. Try this recipe when you want to be a winner! Serve with a Banyuls or a white Saint-Joseph from Chef Pierre's home region of the Rhone.

Ingredients

1 duck
3 ounces butter
1 cup of white wine
2 carrots
2 onions
1 branch of thyme

1 bay leaf
2 lemons
2 teaspoons of lavender honey
7 tablespoons of vinegar
¼ cup oil
salt, pepper

Preparation

TIE the legs on the duck. Sprinkle the duck with salt and pepper. Roast the duck in a 375 degree oven and baste it with a little oil and butter.

IN A very hot saucepan containing the rest of the oil, sauté the wings and neck

CUT the onions and carrots in small dices.

ONCE the wings and neck are golden in color, add the onions, carrots, thyme, bay leaf. Let the mixture reduce and add the white wine and 1 cup of water. Cook for 30 minutes on low.

POUR the honey into a saucepan and let it cook until the color turns to amber, lightly caramelized. Deglaze with the vinegar.

POUR the duck stock through a sieve over the caramel. Let the mixture reduce several minutes.

ADD the lemon juice to the sauce. Whip small pieces of butter into the sauce. Check the seasoning. Cut the duck and serve it with the sauce.

Serves 4

Mousse au Chocolat

The Bon Appetit photographers found our Mousse au chocolat very photogenic. It is appetizing and receives lots of "wows" when it arrives at the table. The tuile can be used as a bowl for fresh berries as well.

Ingredients pate a tuiles

3 ounces of powdered sugar
1⅓ ounce flour
2 eggs

1 ounce butter – room temperature
vanilla
salt

Ingredients mousse au chocolat

½ pound dark chocolate
8 ounces whipped cream

1 ounce sugar
8 ounces egg whites

Preparation pate a tuiles

ADD the powdered sugar to the softened butter by whipping it energetically. Separate the eggs and add the whites to the sugar and butter. Whip well. The mixture should be very well blended. Add the sifted flour, salt, and several drops of vanilla.
BUTTER and flour the baking sheet. Drop a tablespoon of the mixture on the baking sheet and spread it in a circle with a spatula. Cook about 10 minutes in a hot oven.
LOOSEN the circles from the baking sheet and hang them over an upside down bowl to form your tulips.

Preparation mousse au chocolat

SEPARATE the eggs and whip 8 ounces of egg whites in a bowl until stiff. Add the sugar to the egg whites and mix slightly. Melt the chocolate and fold it into the mixture.
WHIP the cream and fold it into the mousse.
REFRIGERATE the mousse at least one hour.

Presentation

On a large plate, pour a strawberry purée decorated with circles of cream. Put an ice cream scoop of chocolate mousse into the baked tulip. Place on the plate and decorate with sprigs of mint and pieces of strawberries.

Serves 4

Monet, Ashland

Replica of covered wagon used on the Oregon Trail.

Broken Top

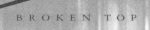

BROKEN TOP

62000 Broken Top Drive
Bend, Oregon
541-383-8200
541-383-1963
www.brokentop.com

Lunch
Tuesday–Friday 11:30 am – 2:00 pm
Dinner
Tuesday–Saturday 6:00 pm – close

Broken Top
David Abell, Chef

I f you would like to experience a romantic evening in one of the most beautiful settings in the world, Broken Top is the ticket. This private, gated community that was voted one of the top five new communities in the nation by the National Association of Home Builders, has at its core a spectacular 27,000 square foot clubhouse that is home to a restaurant open to the public. From the time that you enter through the massive hand-carved wood doors, your eyes are treated to the beauty of the massive great room featuring enormous Douglas fir trusses, massive boulders, and sandalwood stone.

Interior, Broken Top Club.

The plush and comfortable seating arrangements scale down the massiveness and allow you to settle back with a cocktail or refreshment before you begin your dining experience. Depending on the weather, you have the choice of inside or outside dining. Even the inside dining, though, allows you the spectacular views of seven mountain peaks mirrored in the six-acre lake at the base of the clubhouse. While you dine, you can watch the varied waterfowl that use the lake, as well as view the early evening golfers finishing their rounds on the Tom Weiskopf designed golf course.

But, a beautiful setting is not all you have here. Executive Chef David Abell has created an inspiring menu that changes seasonally. Try the Rack of New Zealand Lamb served with a vanilla huckleberry sauce, or the hazelnut crusted loin of rabbit with Gorgonzola raviolis, artichokes and confetti tomatoes. If the bounty of the Northwest is your love, try the roasted salmon marinated in maple syrup and house made mustard, or an appetizer of Dungeness crab cakes crusted with pumpkin seeds and served with grilled baby artichokes, tomatoes, capers, and olives. Broken Top also has a large wine selection and features a wide variety of ports and cognacs to top off your meal, as you watch the sun slide down behind Mt. Bachelor to the west.

Y Wine Spectator Award

Porcini Dusted Wild Salmon
with Seared Foie Gras

Ingredients

4 portions wild salmon about 6 ounces each
1½ tablespoons porcini powder

6 ounces foie gras
3 ounces fresh arugula leaves

Lemon Citronette

juice of 2 lemons
½ cup grape seed oil
½ teaspoon minced shallot

½ teaspoon minced garlic
1 teaspoon Dijon mustard
pinch salt and pepper

Pinot Noir Black Currant Reduction

6 cups Pinot Noir
1 tablespoon black currant purée

Preparation

MAKE the citronette:
COMBINE all ingredients except oil. Using a hand blender, slowly add oil until emulsified. Set aside.

MAKE the Pinot Noir reduction:
ADD wine and purée to non-reactive saucepan and reduce till syrup consistency.

TO ASSEMBLE the dish:
SEASON the salmon filets with salt and pepper. Dust the tops of the filets evenly with porcini powder. Sauté on both sides till just medium, about 3 minutes per side depending on thickness.
SLICE the foie gras into 4 equal slices. Season with salt and pepper and place into a preheated sauté pan and brown on both sides. Be careful not to overcook.
SAUTÉ arugula in a little butter till just wilted. Place in the center of each plate.
TOP the arugula with a portion of salmon topped with a slice of foie gras.
DRIZZLE the foie gras and salmon with the citronette and spoon some of the Pinot reduction around the plate. Serve at once.

Serves 4

SAUTÉED HALIBUT CHEEKS
with Gala Apples and Leeks

Ingredients

- 4 portions halibut cheeks, about 6 ounces each
- 2 gala apples, cored and cut into thin wedges
- 2 cups leek whites, sliced ½ in thick and washed
- 1 teaspoon fresh rosemary lightly chopped
- 1 cup white wine such as a Sauvignon Blanc
- ¼ cup soft unsalted butter
- 1 lemon

Preparation

SEASON cheeks with salt and pepper and lightly dust with flour. Sauté in a little olive oil on both sides till golden, about 5 minutes a side. Remove from pan and keep warm. Add apples, leeks and rosemary to pan. Sauté over medium heat for about 5 minutes or till apples are slightly softened. Deglaze with wine, squeeze in lemon and reduce by half. Stir in butter and season with salt and pepper. Top fish with apple mixture and enjoy.

Serves 4

Dining room, Broken Top Clubhouse.

PEPPERED LOIN OF VENISON
with Ginger Verjus Poached Crispy Sweetbreads, Fig Demi-glace
with Ricotta Salata

Ingredients

1½ pounds venison loin	½ small onion chopped
¾ pound veal sweetbreads	1 stalk celery
1 pint white Verjus	peppercorns
2 ounces sliced ginger	bay leaves

Preparation

For the sweetbreads

THIS may be done a day in advance.

REMOVE the outer membrane from the sweetbreads. In saucepan, combine Verjus, ginger, chopped onion, chopped celery, some black peppercorns, a couple bay leaves and sweetbreads. Bring to boil, reduce heat and simmer for about 20 minutes. Cool sweetbreads in the poaching liquid and refrigerate.

For the venison

MAKE a marinade of 1 cup olive oil, 2 tablespoons good balsamic vinegar, 1 teaspoon minced garlic and 1 tablespoon chopped fresh thyme. Coat venison well and refrigerate overnight.

REMOVE excess marinade from the meat and roll in cracked black pepper and sprinkle with salt. Sear in hot pan with a little oil until browned all around. Roast at 375°F until done, which would be about 125°F internal temperature.

Make the sauce

1 pint Pinot Noir	3 ounces cracked black peppercorns
1 teaspoon minced shallots	1 quart veal stock
1 sprig thyme	½ pound fresh figs

REDUCE wine, shallots, thyme with a few peppercorns until most of the liquid is gone, add veal stock and reduce until sauce coats back of spoon. Strain through fine sieve into another pan. Add quartered figs to sauce and cook for five minutes over low heat. Season with salt and pepper.

To finish

¼ cup crumbled ricotta salata (may substitute Feta)

SLICE sweetbreads about ½ inch thick. Dust with a little flour and sauté on both sides in butter until browned and crispy.

SLICE venison and divide among four plates. Place a slice of crispy sweetbreads on top of each set of sliced meat. Drizzle sauce around plate. Sprinkle with some of the ricotta salata on each and serve.

Broken Top golfcourse.

Cork

150 NW Oregon Ave.
Bend, Oregon
541–382–6881

Tuesday – Saturday
5:00 pm to close

Carin Hill and Greg Unruh

Cork

Carin Hill and Greg Unruh
Proprietors

Carin Hill and Greg Unruh, proprietors of Cork, have selected an appropriate name for their first restaurant venture of their own. With over 150 wines to choose from and 30 wines offered by the glass, it is easy to find the perfect accompaniment to any of the fine offerings on the menu. The soft candlelit atmosphere accented with fresh flowers is a perfect inducement to enjoy a relaxed dining experience.

Carin and Greg have been employed in the restaurant business all their professional lives. They opened Cork in August 2001. Carin handles the "front of the house" and most of the business of running a restaurant, while Greg is responsible for the superb culinary creations that have been described as "American eclectic". Chef Unruh is self-taught, with much of his early experience under a Chinese chef. This influence allowed him to increase and fine-tune his natural ability to blend flavors and ingredients to create eclectic, non-traditional combinations.

This creativity shows itself in such items as the Cork Salad, a combination of fresh greens, sunflower seeds, bleu cheese, corn, and apple with balsamic vinaigrette. Or try the spinach and romaine salad with pumpkin seeds, dried pears, sweet onion, chevre and blood orange vinaigrette.

As for entrees, try the Filet Mignon grilled with a bourbon mustard with toasted shallots, tomato and basil, or the braised lamb shank with a Thai coconut demi-glace and wasabe crushed potato. If you are a seafood lover, you've got to try the scallops served with black sesame pesto and lemon palm sugar glaze or the halibut and clams with ginger kaffir lime cream sauce.

Dining room, Cork.

With exciting dishes such as these, it is no wonder that Cork won the Northwest Palate Magazine's 2002 award for the "Best New Oregon Restaurant" as a result of the Reader's Poll.

Cork's Pappardelle Pasta

Ingredients

1 pound fresh pappardelle pasta
   (2 inch ribbon pasta)
2 large chicken breasts – cut into 2-inch
   squares
2 tablespoons vegetable oil
8 ounces baby prawns (36-50 count/
   pound – peeled and de-veined)
2 jalapeno chiles – chopped
2 ounces white wine

6 ounces orange juice concentrate
6 ounces heavy cream
8 ounces fish stock or clam juice
   salt and pepper
   dashes of hot sauce (tabasco) to taste
2 medium diced tomatoes
¼ cup fresh Parmesan cheese – grated
2 tablespoons fresh basil
2 tablespoons cilantro - chopped

Preparation

IN A large soup or stock pot – boil three quarts of salted water and hold for cooking the pasta.

IN A large sauté or sauce pan – sauté the chicken in vegetable oil over high heat for 3-4 minutes.

ADD prawns and chiles and sauté for one minute.

ADD white wine and reduce for one minute.

ADD orange juice concentrate, cream, stock and seasonings and bring to boil – reduce heat and simmer until slightly thickened – approximately 4-6 minutes.

ADD pasta to boiling water – boil until al dente and strain.

ADD pasta and tomatoes to sauce pan and toss.

SERVE on warm platter or individual pasta bowls.

GARNISH with chopped cilantro and lime segments.

NOTES:
· most flavors of pasta will work with this dish (…egg, spinach, herb, tomato)
· to serve this dish vegetarian – substitute corn, spinach, mushrooms, red peppers…for the chicken and shrimp
· to replace fish stock – 2 extra ounces of cream, 2 ounces of wine and 2 ounces of water

PREPARATION AND COOKING TIME: 40 minutes

Serves 4

Cork's Red Chile Mac 'n Cheese

Ingredients

1 clove of garlic—minced
2 ounces white wine (or beer)
12 ounces heavy cream
4 ounces enchilada sauce
(or ground canned tomatoes seasoned with special spice mix and 2 table-spoons molasses)

1 cup grated cheese - preferably white cheddar (or cheddar, Parmesan, pepperjack...10 ounces dry pasta (Cork uses radiatori)

Preparation

IN A heavy-bottom sauce pan, sauté garlic 2-3 minutes to ignite flavor.

DEGLAZE with wine or beer.

COOK 2 minutes to evaporate alcohol.

ADD remaining ingredients (except cheese).

BRING to a boil.

REDUCE until slightly thickened.

ADD cheese and cooked pasta of choice.

BRING back to a boil.

REDUCE until desired thickness.

Serve and enjoy with grilled chicken, steak, pork or anything off the BBQ, squeezes of fresh lime and lots of great wine.

Gran Marnier Vanilla Bean Cheesecake

Ingredients

For the Crust
    1   10 inch spring-form pan
    ½   butter – melted
    2   cups chocolate cookie crumbs

For the Batter
    27 ounces cream cheese
    2   whole eggs
    4   egg yolks
    1   cup sugar
    1   ounce corn starch

    1   cup heavy cream
    1   vanilla bean – split, scraped and mac-
        erated
    ¼   cup Gran Marnier

Preparation

For the Crust
FOLD chocolate crumbs and melted butter together.
PRESS into spring-form pan until halfway up edges.
BAKE 10 minutes in a 400 degree oven.
RESERVE and hold.

For the Batter
COMBINE vanilla bean with Gran Marnier and macerate for 15 minutes.
WHIP the cream cheese until soft.
ADD whole eggs and yolks and paddle until smooth with no lumps – continuously scraping edges of work bowl.
COMBINE sugar and corn starch - then add to mixture.
ADD cream and blend until smooth.
ADD vanilla / Gran Marnier mixture to batter – paddle until smooth.
POUR cheesecake batter into pre-baked chocolate crust.
SURROUND spring-form pan with double layer of aluminum foil.
PLACE in 4 inch deep baking pan and fill with 2 inches water – bake for approximately 90 minutes - 375 degree oven – until semi-firm – cool 6 hours minimum in refrigerator.

Slice into desired pieces and garnish with mint, chocolate shavings, orange segments, whipped cream..........

Windsurfers on the Columbia River.

Columbia Gorge Hotel

4000 Westcliff Dr.
Hood River, Oregon
541-386-5566
Fax: 541-356-9141
www.columbiagorgehotel.com

7 days a week
Dinner 5:00 – 9:00 pm

Columbia Gorge Hotel
Jeffrey Croke, Chef

A day, an evening, a weekend, or longer; whatever time you have, it will be well spent visiting this historic old hotel overlooking the heart of the Columbia River Gorge. The present hotel was built in 1921 by Simon Benson, an Oregon lumber magnate who had helped to build the Columbia Gorge Scenic Highway and wanted to have a place for tourists to enjoy the fruits of his labor. Robert Rand, who had built a hotel on the sight in 1904, had previously done the layout of the grounds and trails. These grounds were further enhanced by the work of Italian stonemasons brought over to work on the new highway. They built the beautiful stonewalls and bridges that you see today on the property. The 208-foot Wah Gwin Gwin Falls is fed by Phelps Creek that wanders through the property. It is a natural snow-fed creek that begins on the north side of Mt. Hood.

Wander through the beautifully landscaped grounds that are maintained by a Master Gardener and her staff of three full-time employees. From these grounds, you can look down into the gorge to see the many windsurfers far below on the river. The winds blowing up the gorge from the Pacific Ocean create perfect conditions for the sport. Their brightly colored sails sparkle in the summer sunshine as they deftly bob and weave with the winds and the currents. In the winter, the gardens are graced with over 500,000 twinkle lights to brighten the holiday season.

Along with this spectacular setting comes a dining experience that is second to none. The young chef, Jeffrey Croke, came to the hotel in the spring of 2001. After attending the Western Culinary Institute in Portland, he interned for Chef Otto Fennerl at the Trianon Restaurant in Beaverton, earning a promotion to Chef de Cuisine.

You will find an extensive wine list, including the best of the Oregon wineries, as well as Washington, California and international vineyards. The menu runs the gamut of fresh seafood to wild game, with several outstanding salads and appetizers. For a light lunch on the patio or a first course in the formal dining room, try the Merlot Poached Pear Salad. The combination of the sweet walnuts, creamy Gorgonzola, and the shallot-thyme vinaigrette over fresh greens will definitely please your palate. Don't forget to reserve your order of the hotel's signature dessert: Apple Tart Tatin, a delicious pastry filled with caramelized Hood River apples and a vanilla cream Anglaise.

Patio at Columbia Gorge Hotel.

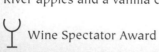 Wine Spectator Award

SEARED BRANDY AND HONEY SCALLOPS

A terrace must. The soft delicate texture of the scallop paired with sweet hints of brandy and honey accompanied with a crispy citrus carrot salad. Paired well with the breath taking views of the Columbia River Gorge.

Ingredients

20 each dry pack sea scallops
2 ounces E&J brandy
2 ounces black currants or gold raisins
½ cup orange juice
2 ounces mayonnaise
2 ounces minced chives
1 ounce minced shallots or yellow onion

2 ounces clover honey
8 ounces shredded carrot salad
½ each lemon juice
1 ounce fresh butter
1 ounce fresh mint
2 ounces extra virgin olive oil

Preparation

Shredded Carrot Salad

SHRED two whole peeled carrots with a mandolin or a standard grater. Mince the mint, zest the orange and lemon, and add to carrots. Add ½ lemon and orange juice to fresh minced mint. Toss mayonnaise and currants into salad.

SEASON the salad with kosher salt and white pepper. Let stand for 15 to 30 minutes so flavors meld.

Scallops

THE PREPARATION of the scallops is relatively simple but you must have your entire mise en place together before you start.

SCALLOPS are very delicate and cook very quickly, if overcooked the texture is unpleasing. To sear scallops start with a very hot pan, no oil. When pan is smoking hot, season the scallops with sea salt and white pepper.

PLACE the dried seasoned scallops in pan with small amount of olive oil. Cook on one side until the scallop starts to release from the pan and turns golden brown, turn carefully. Cook other side for 2 to 3 minutes or until golden brown, add shallots and honey, deglaze with the brandy. Continue cooking until the brandy has flamed out. Finish with fresh butter.

Assembly

TO SERVE place the carrot salad in the center of the plate and surround with the seared scallops drizzle the sauce from the pan on the scallops and garnish with the minced chives

Serves 4

Merlot Poached Pear Salad

Our mixture of wild greens tossed in our house roasted shallot and thyme vinaigrette, laced with spiced caramelized walnuts, and hearty Gorgonzola crumbles. Accompanied with English cumbers and Roma tomatoes.

Poaching Liquid for Pears

½ cup sugar	½ bottle Merlot wine
2 slices of lemon	1 small nub of cleaned ginger
1 tablespoon minced lemon grass	

PLACE pears and all ingredients into thick-bottomed sauce pot and bring to simmer on medium heat. Poach the pears until they are fork tender, about 20 minutes. Remove the pears with a slotted spoon and place on a cooling rack and allow to cool a minimum of 30 minutes before serving.

Ingredients

poached pears	spiced walnuts
mesclun mixed greens	shallot thyme vinaigrette
Gorgonzola cheese	red bell pepper, brunoise (diced and
yellow pear tomatoes	cooked in butter)

Peel and clean firm ripe pears, split in half, remove core and any bruised parts.

For the Shallot Thyme Vinaigrette Dressing

12 clean shallots	1 cup extra virgin olive oil
1 ounce honey	½ bunch fresh thyme
1 tablespoon ground Dijon mustard	¼ cup balsamic vinegar
¼ cup sherry vinegar	½ tablespoon minced garlic
1 teaspoon dry mustard	1 lemon, juiced
pinch of tarragon	

TO ASSEMBLE roast the shallots in the extra virgin olive oil until golden, reserve oil. To make the base for dressing place shallots, mustard, garlic, lemon juice, sherry vinegar, balsamic vinegar, and tarragon in blender and pulse. Once the base has come together add the olive oil until it begins to emulsify starting to look like a creamy well-combined mixture. Taste to see if it needs to be balanced by addition of salt, pepper, or a bit of lemon juice or honey. Chill for 1 hour or for best results over night.

Spiced Hazelnuts Ingredients

½ pound hazelnuts
 1 teaspoon ground white pepper corns
 1 teaspoon ground allspice
½ cup brown sugar
½ cup white sugar

 1 teaspoon cardamom
 1 teaspoon cloves
 1 lemon, juiced
 1 teaspoon cumin powder

ROAST hazelnuts to remove skin. Toss the nuts with the remaining ingredients and roast in the oven until caramelized.

TO ASSEMBLE each salad
FOR each serving use a 5-ounce portion of mesclun mix, ½ poached pear, 1 ounce caramelized walnuts, 1 ounce Gorgonzola cheese-crumbled, 1 ounce shallot thyme vinegar. Toss the salad with the vinaigrette and add half of the walnuts and Gorgonzola cheese until the salad greens are well coated. Place on center of plate. Lay pear core side down and slice the pear from stem to base in ⅛ inch slices until the pear fans out. Place the fanned pear leaning on the salad. Garnish with Gorgonzola cheese, spiced walnuts, yellow pear tomatoes, and brunoise of red bell pepper. Serve immediately.

Serves 6

Entrance, Columbia Gorge Hotel.

Porcini Encrusted Venison Loin
with Raspberry Demi-glace

Ingredients

⅛ cup whole white peppercorns
1 tablespoon whole cumin seeds
1 whole juniper berry
⅛ cup yellow mustard seed
1 bay leaf
⅛ cup fresh rosemary
¼ cup dried morel mushrooms

⅛ cup whole fennel seeds
1 whole clove
⅛ cup dark mustard seed
2 cardamom pods
⅛ cup coriander seeds
¼ cup dried porcini mushrooms
¼ dried chanterelle mushrooms

Preparation

Porcini Spice Rub

PLACE spice rub ingredients (whole white peppercorns, fennel seeds, cumin seeds, clove, juniper berry, dark mustard seed, yellow mustard seed, cardamom pods, bay leaf, coriander seeds, rosemary, and dried mushrooms) on a thin pan and toast on low heat until the whole seeds and herbs begin to release their natural oil and aromatics. Do not over-toast the spices. Cool slightly and grind everything but the bay leaves until a coarse powder is formed. Adjust the seasonings with salt.

CLEAN the venison tenderloin from the rack and remove silver skin. Encrust the meat with the spice rub and pan-sear it in a bit of olive oil. Place in the oven to roast until medium rare. Note: venison is best served medium to medium rare due to the lack of natural fat and marbling.

Raspberry Framboise Demi-Glace

fresh raspberries
Framboise raspberry red wine

veal demi-glace
venison stock

ASSEMBLE the sauce in a small sauce pot by sautéing fresh raspberries, then deglaze with framboise (raspberry wine) and reduced to almost dry au sec. Place equal parts of veal demi-glace and venison stock into the sauce pot with the raspberries. Reduce until the sauce lightly coats the back of a spoon. Finish with a small pat of butter and add salt and pepper to taste.

TO PLATE the venison, slice the tenderloin on the bias into quarter-inch medallions. Place on plate and garnish with fresh raspberries and Gorgonzola cheese. Spoon the sauce over the medallions and cheese.

Serves 4

Hood River Hotel

102 Oak Avenue
Hood River, Oregon
1-800-386-1859
541-386-6090 Fax
www.hoodriverhotel.com

Open Seven Days a week
Breakfast ~ Lunch ~ Dinner
7:00 am-9:00 pm weekends
7:00 am-8:00 pm weekdays

Pasquale's Ristorante at the Hood River Hotel
Chef Mark Whitehead

Chef Mark Whitehead

Located in downtown Hood River, the Hood River Hotel was built in 1913 as an annex to a now fully restored vintage hotel listed on the National Register of Historic Places. The original hotel, the Mt. Hood Hotel built in the 1880's, was located on the corner of the block, serving the transcontinental railroad that operated at the base of the hill below the hotel. The original wood-framed building was demolished in the 1920's. The lobby of the old hotel had been moved to the annex, which faced the Columbia River Scenic Highway that ran directly through the town.

Used as a hotel and rooming house until 1970, the hotel fell into disrepair as so many downtown buildings did in that time. In 1988, Pasquale Barone purchased the hotel, taking 14 months to renovate it with the help of his wife, Jacquie, and local craftspeople. The European charm of the original hotel has been preserved with lofty ceilings, expansive windows and a marble-faced fireplace. In 2000, Brian and Penny Cunninghame purchased the hotel and continue to operate it as an elegant, friendly small town inn.

As part of this building, Pasquale's Ristorante has created a name for itself. Executive Chef Mark Whitehead has developed a special Mediterranean menu with a Northwest style. After graduating from Oregon's Western Culinary Institute in 1986, Mark started his culinary career at the Bahia Resort Hotel in San Diego. Turning his talents to educating others in the culinary skills, Mark spent most of the 1990's as a culinary educator at Linn-Benton Culinary Institute in Albany, Oregon. In 1999, he left the institute to become Chef de Cuisine and then Executive Sous Chef at the prestigious Bay Club at the Kapalua Bay Hotel in Hawaii. In the summer of 2002, Chef Whitehead returned to Oregon to become Executive Chef at Pasquale's Ristorante.

From the Fire-Roasted Calamari with Andouille sausage, sun dried tomatoes and borlotti beans, to the Pomegranate Glazed Salmon with quinoa, grilled Hood River pear, and roasted parsnips, or the Northwest Seafood Paella, you can taste the sunny foods of the Mediterranean in the freshness of his creations.

DUNGENESS CRAB CAKES
Artichoke Tapenade, Garlic Coulis, Caper Berries
Appetizer

Chef Mark Whitehead has featured this crab cake recipe on menus throughout his culinary travels. The crab cake has won numerous awards and because of this we call it the Blue Medal Crab Cake as a joke. The customer enjoys this small bite while sitting in front of the fireplace or dining on the patio in front of The Historic Hood River Hotel.

Ingredients

micro greens
caper berries
3 each large egg

1 cup flour
2 cups panko bread crumbs
canola oil

Crab cakes

10 ounces Dungeness crab meat
8 ounces rock shrimp sautéed and chopped
1 each red bell pepper small diced
½ each sweet onion small diced
1 teaspoon garlic minced
1 cup heavy cream

1 tablespoon Dijon mustard
2 teaspoons worcestershire
¼ cup chopped herbs (tarragon, oregano, Italian parsley)
¼ cup panko (Japanese bread crumbs)
salt and pepper to taste

Garlic coulis

½ pound whole garlic peeled
water to cover garlic

¼ cup extra virgin olive oil
salt to taste

Artichoke tapenade

¾ cup marinated artichokes
¼ cup kalamata olives
1 tablespoon capers
½ teaspoon minced garlic

⅛ cup extra virgin olive oil
1 each lemon, juiced
1 tablespoon basil, chopped
salt and black pepper to taste

Preparation

PLACE the artichokes, kalamata olives, garlic and capers in a food processor and roughly chop. Add the remaining ingredients to artichoke mixture until combined. Season to taste.

ADD the garlic and water together in a saucepan. Bring to a boil and take off the stove and strain. Add new water to the garlic and bring to a boil again. Repeat these steps 10 times replacing the water each time until the garlic is soft and pure white. Strain garlic from the water. Blend the oil and garlic together in a food processor or blender until you get a smooth coulis. Season to taste with salt.

COMBINE onion, red pepper, garlic and cream into a saucepan. Set the pan on medium heat and reduce cream by half. Place cream mixture in the refrigerator to cool. Combine remaining ingredients, including the cream in a bowl and mix together. Season to taste with salt and pepper. Form 4 ounce size cakes and mold together. Refrigerate crab cakes until cool all the way through. Set up a breading station with the flour, egg and bread crumbs. Place the crab cake in the flour and lightly coat. Now add it to the egg until it covers the cake and finally into the panko to finish the breading. Place cakes back into the refrigerator until your oil is heated for frying. Heat enough oil in a pan, so the oil is half way up the crab cake. Cook until the crab cake is golden brown on both sides. Place a pool of garlic coulis on the plate and place the crab cake on the sauce. Top with micro greens and artichoke tapenade. Garnish the plate with caper berries and serve.

Serves 4

Exterior, Hood River Hotel.

Pomegranate Glazed Salmon
Cava Scented Hood River Pear, Roasted Parsnips, Swiss Chard

The menu at Pasquale's restaurant will always have a featured seasonal salmon dish. The fall season allows us to add the local pear to this dish. The combination of the pomegranate, parsnips and swiss chard makes this a dish to savor as winter is fast approaching.

Ingredients

28 ounces salmon cut into 7 ounce portions	1 bunch swiss chard
	2 each parsnips

Poached Hood River Pear

2 each Bartlett pear peeled, cut in half and cored	1 each cinnamon stick
1 cup sparkling wine (Spanish cava)	1 each star anise
1 cup water	3 each black peppercorn
¼ cup sugar	1 each lemon juiced

Pomegranate Glaze

1 cup pomegranate syrup	⅛ cup honey
¼ cup fresh orange juice	¼ cup poaching liquid

Preparation

MIX the water, sparkling wine, sugar and spices in a saucepan. Bring to a simmer until the sugar has dissolved. Place the pears into the liquid and turn temperature down low. Poach pears until tender and pull off the heat and let cool in the poaching liquid.

MIX all the ingredients together for the pomegranate glaze in a saucepan and bring to a simmer. Simmer until the glaze coats the back of a spoon. Cool and reserve for later.

SEASON the salmon filets with salt and pepper. Place a fry pan on the stove and heat on medium high heat. Add a couple of tablespoons of oil to the pan. Place the salmon skin side up in the hot pan and sear in the oil until golden brown. Flip the salmon over and lower the heat. Towards the end add the glaze and let the salmon braise in the glaze. Be careful of your heat and add a little more of the poaching liquid to finish the glazing of the salmon. Place salmon on the plate and serve with the scented pear. Parsnips and swiss chard are nice accompaniments with this dish.

Serves 4

Paella Rice

Paella: (pie-ay-yuh) (noun) 1. A technique for making rice dishes. The word paella comes from the Latin word patella meaning pan. The only indispensable ingredients are rice, water, and olive oil. Everything else is the subject of endless debate. Paella's are as free spirited as the chefs who create them. Once the techniques are mastered, the sky's the limit.

Ingredients

2 tablespoon olive oil	1½ cups paella rice (Spanish medium
1 teaspoon garlic	grained)
½ each onion small diced	2½ cups vegetable stock
1 stalk celery small diced	2 teaspoons saffron
1 each red pepper small diced	salt and pepper to taste
1 each bay leaf	

Preparation

HEAT the oil in a pan. Add the vegetables and sauté until they are tender. Add the rice and stir until the rice is coated with the oil. Add the stock, saffron and bay leaf. Bring to a simmer, reduce heat and cover with the lid. Simmer rice for 25 minutes until the liquid has been absorbed and the rice is tender. Season to taste with salt and pepper. Finish the rice by drizzling olive oil over the top. This dish can be combined with many different items to make it a entrée. At the restaurant, we feature a seafood paella with shrimp, salmon, crab.

Serves 4

Mt Hood Railroad Co Depot and train.

Stonehedge Gardens

3405 Cascade
Hood River, Oregon
541-386-3940
www.stonehedgegardens.com

Open Daily For Dinner
5:00 pm to close

Stonehedge Gardens
Mike & Shawna Caldwell, Owners

As you wind up the narrow path through part of the six heavily wooded acres that comprise Stonehedge Gardens, you begin to realize you are headed for an unusual dining experience in a romantic setting. Originally built in 1898 by the Portland Skene family as a summer getaway, the house has served as an exceptional restaurant for over 25 years. Mike and Shawna Caldwell are the current owners, having bought the Inn in 2000. Mike had served as a prep cook at the Inn during his high school years when it was owned by Jean Harmon, one of his teachers at Hood River Valley High School.

Previous to buying Stonehedge, Mike had served as the Maitre D' at the prestigious Columbia Gorge Hotel and then as Cellarmaster at Flerchinger Vineyards. He and Shawna had also purchased and continue to operate the North Oak Brasserie in downtown Hood River.

The old Inn has several intimate dining rooms, including the Sun Porch, Library, Wine Cellar and Grand Room with fireplace. But if you really want a romantic dinner, and the weather is permitting, ask to be seated on the lantern-lit massive patio. Consisting of over 6,000 square feet of Italian stone, the patio can seat up to 200 people. However, because of the excellent design, consisting of five different levels, each table has an intimate feel. Dining under the canopy of the massive old trees that fill the property lends a special relaxed atmosphere to the dinner.

Mike and Shawna Caldwell

Start your dinner with an appetizing starter such as the Escargot served with butter, garlic, brandy and cream in a puff pastry. Or try the refreshing House Salad of organic field greens with spiced pecans, mandarin oranges and spiced pecan vinaigrette. Then move on to the Coconut Crusted Chicken seared in olive oil and served with lime butter or the Sambuca Shrimp: large gulf prawns, prepared with dried peppers, licorice liquor, and anise butter. But save room for the house specialty, a Flaming Bread Pudding using their cinnamon baked baguette bread topped with crème brulee.

ROASTED LEG OF LAMB
with Pumpkin Hash and Crabapple-Mint Au Jus

Every year around harvest time in the Hood River Valley, Stonehedge Gardens has a Pumpkin and Pinot Festival. This recipe is one of the favorites from that menu. We make our own crabapple-mint jelly, but you could (and I would recommend) buying a prepared apple-mint jelly from your store.

Ingredients

Roasted Leg of Lamb
8 cloves of garlic, roasted
2 tablespoons rosemary, chopped
2 tablespoons olive oil
1 tablespoon Dijon mustard

salt and pepper, to taste
1 leg of lamb, boned and tied
2 tablespoons olive oil

Pumpkin Hash
1 medium-sized pumpkin, seeded and peeled
2 baking potatoes
4 slices thick bacon, chopped

2 tablespoons garlic, chopped
salt and pepper, to taste
¼ cup bread crumbs

Crab Apple-Mint Au Jus
2 tablespoons butter
1 shallot, chopped
1 tablespoon flour

2 tablespoons sherry
3 cup beef consommé
½ cup apple-mint jelly

Preparation

For the Roasted Leg of Lamb
COMBINE the garlic, rosemary, olive oil, Dijon, salt and pepper until it forms a paste. Rub the paste over the leg of lamb and marinate, refrigerated, for several hour or overnight.

REMOVE from the refrigerator 30 minutes before cooking. Heat oven to 350 degrees F.

HEAT 2 tablespoons olive oil over medium-high heat in a pan large enough to hold the leg of lamb. When oil is hot, add the leg of lamb and sear each side until well browned. Transfer to the oven and cook until the internal temperature is 135 degrees F., approximately 20-30 minutes. Allow to rest 10 minutes before slicing.

For the Pumpkin Hash
CUT the pumpkin and potatoes into ½-inch cubes. Roast in a preheated 350 degree F. oven until cooked through, about 20 minutes.

SAUTÉ bacon over medium heat in a large sauté pan until brown. Do not drain the fat. Add the garlic, pumpkin and potatoes, and sauté until slightly crisp and browned. Season with salt and pepper. Mix in the bread crumbs until the pumpkin hash is coated. Keep warm until ready to assemble.

For the Crabapple-Mint Au Jus

HEAT butter in a sauce pan over medium heat. Add shallot and cook until lightly browned. Add flour and cook, stirring, until mixture begins to turn brown, about 4 minutes. Whisk in sherry, consommé and jelly. Bring to a boil; reduce heat and simmer for 5 minutes.

To Assemble

ON A large heated platter, place the Pumpkin Hash. Slice the lamb into ½-inch slices and arrange the slices, overlapping, on the hash. Spoon the au jus over the lamb, and serve more on the side, to be passed at the table.

A wedding celebration at Stonehedge Gardens.

PORTOBELLO MUSHROOM RAVIOLI
with Hood River Pears and Walnuts

Ingredients

1   pound fresh mushroom ravioli
2   tablespoon olive oil
½   medium red onion, sliced
1   Hood River pear, cored and diced
¼   cup currants
1   tablespoon chopped garlic

¼   cup sherry
1   tablespoon balsamic vinegar
3   tablespoon butter
    salt and pepper, to taste
¼   cup walnuts, toasted and chopped

Preparation

COOK ravioli according to the directions on the package.

WHILE ravioli's are cooking, heat olive oil in sauté pan over medium heat. Add red onions and cook until lightly browned; add pears and currants. Continue to sauté for 2 more minutes. Add garlic to the onion-pear mixture. Cook for 1 minute; do not let the garlic brown. Add the sherry and balsamic vinegar; reduce slightly. Remove from the heat and stir in the butter until well-incorporated. Season with salt and pepper.

ADD the cooked ravioli to the onion-pear sauce and return to the heat. Simmer for one minute. Arrange the ravioli on a heated platter, spoon sauce over the ravioli, and top with the walnuts.

Serves 4 as an appetizer or 2 as an entrée.

ORGANIC GREENS
with Spiced-Pecan Vinaigrette and Mandarin Oranges

This salad began at our Cajun restaurant, The Big Easy, but everyone loved it so much that we made it our house salad at Stonehedge Gardens.

Ingredients

- 1 *pound organic mesclun mix*
- ⅓ *cup Spiced-Pecan Vinaigrette (recipe follows)*
- ¼ *cup Spiced Pecans, chopped (recipe follows)*
- ¼ *cup mandarin oranges, drained*

TOSS the mesclun mix with the vinaigrette. Top with the chopped pecans and mandarin oranges.

For the Spiced Pecans

- ½ *pound brown sugar*
- ¼ *cup cinnamon*
- ¼ *cup cumin*
- ¼ *cup kosher salt*
- 2 *tablespoons ginger*
- 2 *tablespoons cayenne*
- 2 *tablespoons garlic powder*
- 1 *tablespoon mace*
- 1 *egg white*
- 4 *cup pecans*

HEAT oven to 350 degrees F. Beat egg white until fluffy; mix in ¼ cup water. Toss pecans with egg white mix. Season with ½ cup seasoning. Bake approximately 20 minutes, or until crisp.

For the Spiced-Pecan Vinaigrette

- 2 *cups spiced pecans*
- ¼ *cup minced garlic*
- 3 *ounces stone ground mustard*
- 1½ *cups dark brown sugar*
- 2 *teaspoons kosher salt*
- 2 *teaspoons black pepper*
- 1 *cup balsamic vinegar*
- ½ *cup red wine vinegar*
- 3 *cup oil*

PLACE pecans in a food processor and pulse until pecans are coarsely chopped. Add all the other ingredients except for the oil; purée. With the processor running, add the oil in a thin stream until all the oil is incorporated. Refrigerate until ready to use.

Baldwin Saloon

Historic Restaurant & Bar

205 Court Street
The Dalles, Oregon
541-296-5666

Monday – Thursday
11:00 am – 9:00 pm
Friday and Saturday
11:00 am– 10:00 pm

The Baldwin Saloon
Mark and Tracy Linebarger, Owners

In 1876, James and John Baldwin opened the original Baldwin Saloon, and its proximity to the railroad and Columbia River made it a busy, successful enterprise. After the Baldwin brothers, Dr. Charles Allen took over. Doctor, only by virtue of the fact he adopted the title, Allen commissioned a cast iron façade from Golden State Iron Works in San Francisco, complete with medical insignias. A brothel flourished in a small, attached building behind the saloon for the term of Charles Allen's ownership. Subsequent businesses such as a steamboat navigational office, warehouse, coffin storage site, and restaurant followed.

In 1962 the building became the Bonney Saddle Shop, which it remained for the next 30 years until the Bonneys retired and sold the place to Mark and Tracy Linebarger. Their dream was to return the building to its roots as a restaurant and bar. The renovation was extensive, requiring the basement to undergo a complete remodel to become a commercial kitchen, and took a year of backbreaking effort. On December 15, 1991, the revitalized Baldwin Saloon opened for business. The restaurant echoes the past but doesn't repeat it, offering a more genteel atmosphere than its predecessor. The original brick walls and old fir floor serve as the ideal backdrop for the mahogany and golden oak booths, brass fixtures and turn-of-the-century oil paintings. The 18-foot long mahogany back bar, made in the 1900s, has large columns with scrollwork and a mirror trimmed with stained glass panels.

The menu features fresh meats, seafood and oyster dishes, as well as sandwiches and burgers. The soups, salads, breads, and desserts are made on the premises. In good weather, guests enjoy dining outside on the cedar deck, and during the weekends, the 1894 Schubert mahogany piano provides tunes and memories of yesteryear. The Baldwin Saloon is a culinary treat and a historic delight.

Ferry Hood River — White Salmon.

STUFFED DATES WITH CHERVE
Appetizer

Ingredients

6 dates, pitted
3 slices bacon, cut In half
chevre cheese

softened apple, quartered
sliced grapes
green leaf lettuce

Preparation

STUFF the dates (with a pastry bag with a small plain tip) with the goat cheese. Wrap the date with ¼ slice of bacon and pick it with the toothpick. Bake in a 350 degree oven for about 12 to 15 minutes, turning over at least once. Served on a small plate with a garnish of apple and grapes on a green leaf.

Serves 1

BASIL AND TOMATO COUSCOUS

Ingredients

2 cups cooked couscous
(cooked to package instructions, use chicken stock and not water)
2 medium romas tomatoes, medium diced
1 small red onion, medium diced
3 tablespoons fresh basil, thinly sliced
2 tablespoons sugar
1 tablespoon chopped fresh parsley

½ tablespoon chopped fresh garlic
2 tablespoons red wine vinegar
1 tablespoon olive oil
salt and fresh ground black pepper to taste
1 tablespoon chicken stock
1 teaspoon fresh lemon juice

MIX all the ingredients, except the chicken stock, lemon juice, and the cooked couscous. Let sauce marinate at least a couple of hours, can be stored over night in the refrigerator, covered. Sauté the mixture for a few minutes on medium heat, add the chicken stock and lemon juice and reduce down for just minute or two. Add the couscous and stir and let the mixture be absorb. Serve hot .

Serves 6 to 8

Hazelnut Salmon

This recipe brings together three of the best that Oregon has to offer; salmon, hazelnuts and marionberries. The sauce can be made a week ahead and stored in the refrigerator. The salmon can be breaded ahead of time, too.

Ingredients

1   7 ounce salmon fillet
   flour, to coat
   hazelnuts, blanched, finely chopped
   breading, ground

egg wash, to coat
butter
marionberry sauce

Preparation

DUST the salmon In the dour and dip in the egg wash. Bread in a mixture of ½ hazelnuts and ½ breading. Brown off in a sautéed pan with butter and put on a, baking plate into a 350 degree oven for about 15 minutes. Serve with the marionberry sauce on the side.

For the Marionberry Sauce

¼   cup shallot, chopped
1   cup red wine vinegar or raspberry
   vinegar
5½   pounds marionberries or blackberries

water, to cover
¾   cup sugar, add more or less
   cornstarch, to thicken

DO A reduction with the shallots and red wine vinegar, until the liquid is almost gone. Add the berries and water and bring to a boil. Add the sugar and adjust the sweetness. Reduce the heat down and thicken with cornstarch and water, until it's a thick syrup texture. Strain the seed out and refrigerate the sauce until ready to use.

Serves 1

PEANUT BUTTER PIE

This peanut butter pie recipe had its start back in the mid-70's, when I worked at Jake's Famous Crawfish. We did a grand opening for a radio station owned by Gene Autry. He sent a pie recipe to us and it was the best recipe for peanut butter pie that anyone had tried. Since then, I've changed a few things, such as the crust and chocolate topping, but the filling is pretty much the same. I could not improve on it. The pie freezes well, without the topping.

Ingredients

3 pounds cream cheese, softened
4 pounds peanut butter, creamy
6 cups sugar

6 ounces butter, melted and cooled
6 cups heavy cream, whipped
6 tablespoons vanilla

Preparation

CREAM the cream cheese, add the sugar slowly. Add the peanut butter and vanilla, whip until smooth. Add the butter and whip until blended. Fold in the whipped cream and spoon into pre-baked pie shells and refrigerate overnight. Top with ganache and refrigerate.
Cut in 12.

For the Pie Crust

¾ cup graham cracker crumbs
¾ cup chocolate wafer cookie crumbs

¼ cup sugar
⅓ cup butter, melted

COMBINE the crumbs with the sugar and add the butter. Pat into pie pan and bake at 350° for 8 minutes. Cool, before filling with the peanut butter mixture,

Serves 5

Going out to find land for homesteaders.

Hotel Condon

202 S. Main
Condon, Oregon
541-384-4624
www.hotelcondon.com

Lunch
11:00 am till the dining room closes
Dinner
5:00 – 8:00 pm Sunday-Thursday
and 9:00 pm Friday and Saturday

Hotel Condon
John Thompson, Executive Chef

Fireplace at Hotel Condon.

In the heart of the high-desert wheat country is the tiny town of Condon, which hosts the historic Hotel Condon. The famous John Day River basin with its premier fishing is not far away. Built in the 1920's, the hotel has recently been renovated by a group of investors that have beautifully rejuvenated the three-story building. Built on the corner of Gilliam and Main Streets, the hotel features welcoming red swinging doors. Originally containing 42 rooms with shared bathrooms, the renovation has produced 18 comfortably private rooms with many modern amenities. A special extra is a 2nd floor private lounge for guests that includes a fireplace and comfy chairs for reading or relaxing. Guests are served a complimentary Continental Breakfast

The Sage Lounge features a replica of a 1900 saloon bar from the Buckhorn Saloon, and the dining room hosts a fireplace burning aromatic juniper wood, comfortably upholstered dining chairs, white linen service, and beautiful stained glass windows.

In August 2003, Chef John Thompson joined the Condon Hotel staff and has created an intriguing menu of old favorites with new exciting additions. For an appetizer, try the Locust Grove Mushrooms, stuffed and baked with crab, shrimp and blue cheese. Or try the Alkali Flats Deep Fried Brie in Pastry, served with marionberry compote. The Hay Creek Salmon, seared with fresh herbs and panko, and served with a light daphnia blue cheese sauce is exceptional, as are the steaks that are served with a brown chili demi-glace.

Comfortable seating at Hotel Condon.

Although Condon is far from the fast-paced tourism of today's interstate highways, take the time to visit this friendly community and you will be rewarded with a rich and relaxing experience.

COCONUT HAWAIIAN SHRIMP
with Brandied Orange Marmalade
Appetizer

Ingredients

6 U16/U20 shrimp (peeled and deveined)
1 cup shredded coconut
2 cups flour (sifted)
4 eggs
1 cup orange marmalade
1 ounce brandy

1 teaspoon vanilla extract
½ cup heavy cream
½ cup half & half
2 cups canola oil
1 sprig fresh mint

Preparation

For the Batter
COMBINE flour, heavy cream, half & half, and vanilla extract. Blend until smooth.

Brandied Marmalade: Turn brandy into Marmalade.

For the Shrimp
DRY shrimp thoroughly. Dip in batter, coat with coconut and fry in canola oil until golden brown. 1½ minutes maximum.

PLATE fried shrimp. Top with dabs of orange marmalade and garnish with mint.

Recommended Wine: Your favorite Pinot Gris

Makes one appetizer

DEVIL'S GAP JUMBO SHRIMP DIABLO

Ingredients

5   u10/u15 shrimp (peeled and de veined)
8   ounces linguini (cooked)
2   tablespoons pinon pesto
¼   cup red peppers (julienne)
¼   cup heavy cream
1   teaspoon crushed red chilies

¼   cup zucchini, yellow squash, and
     carrots (julienne)
½   teaspoon fresh basil (chopped)
2   cloves garlic (chopped)
½   cup shredded Parmesan
½   cup olive oil

Preparation

IN A sauté pan over medium heat, combine olive oil and shrimp till almost done. Add garlic, red chilies, peppers, vegetables, and heavy cream. Bring to a slow simmer. Add Parmesan, pesto, and linguini, moving pan consistently until hot. Separate shrimp before plating.

TRANSFER remaining contents of sauté pan to the plate. Place shrimp on top and garnish with a bit of parsley and Parmesan.

** Can substitute chicken

Recommended Wine: Your favorite Chardonnay

Serves 1

SISSY'S CONDON CLAM CHOWDER

Ingredients

5-6 medium potatoes (peeled & diced)
2 medium onions (diced)
1 tablespoon garlic (minced)
8 ounces clam base
16 ounces butter (unsalted and melted)
16 ounces flour
2 cups heavy cream

1 cup half & half
48 ounces canned clams with juice
1 tablespoon thyme (ground)
2 tablespoons vegetable oil
4 quarts water
½ cup parsley (chopped)

Preparation

Roux

IN A small saucepan, melt butter and add flour. Mix till smooth.

Body

IN A heavy pot, combine oil, onions, and garlic. Sauté over low heat till onions are transparent. Add water, potatoes, and clam base. Cook at a roiling boil till potatoes are almost done. Add roux. Cook at roiling boil for 10 –15 minutes, stir frequently. Add heavy cream, half & half, thyme, and clams with juice. Stir to mix and heat through. Reduce heat to serving temperature. Add parsley.

FILL soup bowl with chowder and place crackers on the side. Offer fresh ground pepper.

Recipe produces 1½ gallon

BAKED JOHN DAY DUCK
with Garlic Madeira Butter

Ingredients

8-12 *ounce duck breast*
1 *cup wild rice*
3 *cleaned shiitake mushrooms*
  (sautéed whole)

⅛ *pound unsalted butter*
1 *teaspoon chopped parsley*
1 *clove fresh garlic*
½ *ounce Madeira*

Preparation

For the Garlic Madeira Butter
IN A mixer at low speed combine butter (unsalted), chopped garlic, parsley, & Madeira. Stir consistently until whipped and blended and then freeze.

For the Duck Breast
TENDERIZE an 8-12 ounce duck breast, roll cooked rice and Madeira butter inside. Bake at 275° for 45 minutes.

**Fresh chicken or pheasant breast may be substituted for duck.

PLACE three shiitakes on plate, cover with breast and 2 slices Madeira butter vegetable of your choice to the side.

Recommended Wine: Your favorite Cotes d`Rhone

Serves 1

Raphael's Restaurant

233 SE 4th St.
Pendleton, Oregon
541-276-8500
800-944-CHEF
www.raphaelsrestaurant.com

June 1st - September 15th
Tuesday-Saturday 5:00-9:00 pm
September 16th - May 31st
Tuesday-Thursday 5:00-8:00 pm
Friday-Saturday 5:00-9:00 pm

Raphael's Restaurant
& Catering Inc.

Chef Rob and Raphael Hoffman
Proprietors

Raphael and Rob Hoffman have created a luxurious dining atmosphere in a beautiful historic house in Pendleton. The graceful Queen Anne style house has a long history. Thought to have been built in 1904, it was discovered during renovations following a fire, that it originally was built by a pioneer woman raising three children in 1876.

After passing through several owners in its early history, it was purchased by Colonel J.H. Raley, a highly respected member of Pendleton's early society, serving as state senator, judge, and cattle rancher. His son, Roy, occupied the house after the death of his father in 1936. Roy was the driving force behind the creation of the famous Pendleton Round-Up, serving as its first president in 1910.

In 1991, the Hoffman's bought the home and transformed it into their restaurant and living quarters. They had originally operated their restaurant at the Pendleton airport. The home seems to have been built for entertaining, with large luxurious rooms amply trimmed with mahogany and oak and lead glass windows.

As you enter the restaurant, you will see a beautiful spindled oak staircase with a rawhide and metal teepee chandelier depicting a Native American buffalo hunt. The many Native American touches throughout the building are the inspiration of Raphael, a member of the Nez Perce tribe.

While Raphael greets and visits with guests, Rob is the Chef and creator of the sumptuous dinner menu. The Northwest is the place to enjoy salmon, and a better presentation than Rob's Indian Salmon would be hard to find. The native wild huckleberries used in the puree are the perfect accompaniment to this rich seafood.

Each month, Chef Rob features special entrees. January diners will be treated with dishes featuring Dungeness crab, while July and August visitors will enjoy Western Barbecue entrees. And, for those who love wild game specialties, the months of October and November feature such delights as Rocky Mountain elk osso buco, rattlesnake and rabbit sausage.

Raphael's Restaurant, Pendleton

Indian Salmon

Ingredients

8 ounce salmon filet (skin off)
1 shallot diced fine
3 thin tomato slices
1½ ounces fresh spinach leaves

1 tablespoon butter
2 cups dry vermouth
1 tablespoon huckleberry purée

Preparation

MELT butter in sauté pan or skillet, then add salmon sprinkled with diced shallots. Top with tomato slices and cover with spinach leaves. Place over medium heat, add vermouth then cover and simmer for approximately 10 minutes (depending upon the thickness of the filet).

REMOVE spinach covered salmon fillet from pan; place on plate and top with huckleberry purée.

For the Huckleberry Purée

1 cup huckleberries
(blackberries or marionberry, or raspberries could be substituted)

2 tablespoons sugar
1 teaspoon arrowroot
¼ cup water

PLACE huckleberries and water in a blender and purée. In a small saucepan bring to a boil, then mix arrowroot and sugar in a small bowl and add to boiling purée. Mix well then cook to room temperature

Serves 1

GREEK PASTA

Ingredients

2 ounces butter
6 ounces boneless skinless chicken breast
(cut into small strips)
5 mushrooms (cut into halves)
1 ounce sliced red bell pepper
1½ ounces sliced red onions
1 ounce fresh spinach leaves

1 ounces diced tomatoes
6 ounces cooked fettuccini or linguini
pasta
1 ounce fresh grated Parmesan cheese
(myzithra cheese also works well)
1 teaspoon Lawreys seasoning or to taste

Preparation

PLACE butter in sauté pan on high heat and cook until well browned. Add chicken, mushrooms, onions, and peppers, then sauté until chicken is fully cooked. Add fettuccini pasta, diced tomatoes, and spinach. Cover for about one minute to wilt spinach, remove lid then toss with fresh Parmesan cheese and season to taste. This recipe also works well with beef.

Serves 1 or 2

PASTA SALAD

Ingredients

1 pound cooked penne pasta
¼ cup diced onions
¼ pound red bell peppers cut in fine strips
3 stalks sliced celery

1 can pitted black olives
½ pound broccoli florets
3 ounces fresh grated Parmesan cheese
1½ cups balsamic vinaigrette dressing

TOSS all ingredients in large bowl

For the Balsamic Vinaigrette Dressing

1 cup balsamic vinegar
1 cup peanut oil
1 garlic clove chopped extra fine
1 ounce onion chopped extra fine
1 ounce green bell pepper diced extra fine
1 teaspoon whole basil

1 teaspoon black pepper
1 teaspoon garlic salt
1 ounce sun dried tomato crumbles
¼ cup water
¼ cup sugar

PLACE all ingredients in mixing bowl except peanut oil and mix well then slowly whisk in peanut oil. Serve over salad.

Serves about 10

Chef Rob's Sautéed Wild Mushrooms

Ingredients

2 ounces butter
¼ cup sherry
1 tablespoon sour cream
½ cup whipping cream
½ teaspoon garlic seasoning

2 teaspoon Lawreys seasoning
12 assorted mushrooms button, shiitake, portobello, others such as morels and chanterelles may be substituted.

Preparation

SAUTÉ mushrooms in butter until tender then add sherry, sour cream and whipping cream Then simmer until sour cream blends in and sauce starts to thicken. If the sauce starts to break then you can bring it back together by adding a little more whipping cream.

Serves 4

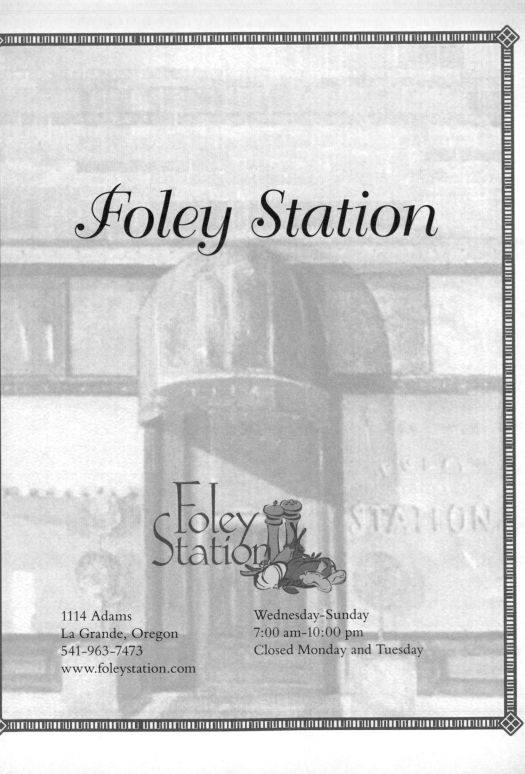

Foley Station

1114 Adams
La Grande, Oregon
541-963-7473
www.foleystation.com

Wednesday–Sunday
7:00 am–10:00 pm
Closed Monday and Tuesday

Foley Station
Merlyn Baker, Chef

Entrance, Foley Staion.

The beautiful eastern Oregon Grande Rhonde River Valley hosts the welcoming little town of La Grande. A drive through the town's streets will leave you envying the pleasant lifestyle of this friendly town. And, if you happen to be in the mood to enjoy an innovative meal, stop in at Foley Station, where Chef Merlyn Baker will be sure to liven your taste buds with one of his creations.

Long a fixture of downtown La Grande, the restaurant opened in its new location in December 2003. The new location is in the Charles Palmer Building that was built in 1892. Its early history included use as a furniture and bedding store, and then a book and stationary store that supplied the first phonographs sold in La Grande. When the Foley Station crew purchased the building in August 2003, they decided to bring back the uniqueness of this historical building. The interior was fully remodeled, exposing the original brick, and refurbishing the pressed tin ceilings. The stonewalls of the foundation, laid by Chinese masons in 1892, were exposed to create a Mediterranean wine cellar atmosphere. In the basement, a fire-lit grotto is the centerpiece for banquet facilities. The main dining room is designed around an open kitchen with additional seating at the dining counter and bar.

As a tourist enjoying a meal at Foley Station for the first time, you feel that you are drawn into the lifeblood of the town. The smell of fresh baked bread greets you as you enter, and it's quite obvious that the restaurant draws a large crowd of "regulars" that are happy to let you know what they like about Foley Station and La Grande. Chef Baker's menu can only be described as eclectic. Along with the wonderful Northwestern fare, you will find dishes with accents from Asian, Greek, Basque, Italian, and Cajun cooking – and all done superbly. An international wine list and a full bar compliment the epicurean experience. But, if you want the best lemonade you've ever had, try one of their four fresh squeezed flavors. The ginger lemonade is outstanding; made from their own ginger syrup recipe.

Northwest Forest Mushroom and Oregon Hazelnut Strudel
Appetizer

Our strudel is always popular when it is on the menu, sweet or savory. Our menus are ever changing so you may find this item or one of many other inciting palate pleasers to satisfy you. Chef Merlyn suggests Canoe Ridge 1999 Cabernet Sauvignon with this appetizer.

Ingredients

1 pound assorted forest mushrooms
2 teaspoons shallots, minced
2 teaspoons garlic, minced
3 tablespoons butter
1 tablespoon lemon Juice
3 tablespoons dry sherry
4 teaspoons white wine

1 cup heavy cream
2¼ cup hazelnuts, toasted and coarsely chopped,
1 cup freshly grated Parmesan cheese
¼ teaspoon salt
¼ teaspoon black pepper

Ingredients for the Strudel Dough

¾ cups lukewarm water
1 large egg, beaten
¼ teaspoon white vinegar

2½ cups bread flour
¾ teaspoons salt
2 tablespoons melted butter

Preparation

PREPARE the strudel dough. Combine the water, egg, salt and vinegar mixing well.
PLACE the flour in a mixing bowl, add half of the liquid and mix a few seconds.
ADD remaining liquid and continue to mix until smooth, about 1 minute.
ADD the melted butter, mix until blended.
KNEAD the dough slightly by hand to check for consistancy.
COAT with a drop of oil and place in a covered bowl.
ALLOW the dough to sit at room temperature for 30 minutes before using.

COMBINE ¼ cup toasted hazelnuts and ¼ cup grated Parmesan cheese. Reserve this mixture to use in rolling the strudel.
MINCE the assorted mushrooms.
SAUTÉ the shallots and garlic in butter until lightly toasted.
ADD the mushrooms and lemon juice, continue to cook until the liquid from the mushrooms has evaporated.

ADD the white wine and sherry to the hot pan and stir in to the mushrooms.

ADD the cream, salt and pepper. Reduce the liquid by half and add the remaining cheese and hazelnuts.

PLACE in a shallow pan to cool.

STRETCH the strudel dough. Butter lightly with drawn butter.

PLACE the cooled filling at one end of the dough and roll as per all strudel preparations, brushing each turn of dough with drawn butter and sprinkling with the reserved hazelnut/Parmesan mixture.

BAKE at 400° F for approximately 25 minutes.

COOL slightly before slicing.

Serves approximately 4

Sesame Seared Scallops
with Roasted Garlic and Lemon Grass Sauce

This recipe has been a signature item on Foley Station's dinner menu since 1997. Although each month our menu changes to reflect seasonal and regional food items this signature preparation returns to the menu each spring or summer for about three months, much to the relief of regular guests.

Ingredients

6 each 6 dry pack ocean scallops U-20 size or larger

2 cups flour seasoned with white pepper, salt and granulated garlic

2 cups egg wash
(a mixture of one egg and one cup milk)

¼ cup black and white sesame seeds, combined

2 cups panko bread crumbs
sesame oil for frying

Preparation

DREDGE the scallops in seasoned flour.

DIP the scallops in the egg wash.

DIP one of the flat sides of the scallops in the sesame seeds then place in the panko bread crumbs, coating the scallop with crumbs.

COAT a medium-hot sauté pan with sesame oil, add the scallops, seed side down, and fry approximately 1 minute. Turn the scallops and continue frying for an additional minute. Cooking time will very depending on size of scallops, heat of pan and desired doneness. Over cooking will cause the crust to fall off and create a tough scallop.

SERVE the scallops with Roasted Garlic Lemon Grass Sauce. A nice accompaniment may include jasmine rice steamed with split baby garbanzo beans and daikon radish seeds and a vegetable of fresh shiitake mushroom caps stir fried in sesame oil and splashed with rice wine.

Please note: the importance of dry-pack scallops cannot be overstated.

For the Roasted Garlic Lemon Grass Sauce
Makes about 2 cups

1 cup dry white wine	2 teaspoons roasted garlic, crushed
¼ cup rice wine vinegar	1 inch thin sliced fresh lemon grass
2 tablespoons lemon juice	2 cups coconut milk
1½ teaspoons cracked black pepper	1 pound cold unsalted butter
1 tablespoon minced shallots	

COMBINE the wine, vinegar, lemon juice, pepper, shallots and lemon grass in a non-corrosive saucepan. Bring to a simmer. Cooking over medium reduce to a syrup.

ADD 2 tablespoons of water, the coconut milk and garlic to the syrup. Continue to cook reducing the liquid by ⅓.

WHILE the liquid is still boiling stir in the cold butter a few pieces at a time, constantly stirring until all of the butter is melted.

IMMEDIATELY remove from the heat and strain into a warm bowl. Serve this sauce with sesame-seared scallops.

Serves 8-12

Wine suggestion: Trimbach 1999 Gewurztraminer (Alsace) with the Sesame Scallops!

CARROT-GINGER BISQUE
soup

Diversity is key with Foley Station - art, music, décor and menus. On Wednesdays we provide an excellent selection of vegetarian specials in addition to our regular menu. This soup is usually served on a Wednesday but is requested throughout the week and loved by all. Very nice with Zenato 2001 Pinot Grigio (Italy) and a fresh pear and blue cheese salad.

Ingredients

1 tablespoon fresh ginger, peeled and grated	½ teaspoon honey
1 pound carrots, peeled and rough cut	2½ cups water
¾ cup onion, peeled and diced	2 cups heavy cream
3 tablespoons butter	2 cups half & half
2 cups light chicken stock	2 tablespoons sherry
	salt and white pepper to taste

Preparation

IN A heavy soup pot, place the butter, ginger, carrots, and onion.

STEW vegetables in the butter over a medium heat for about 10 minutes.

ADD the chicken stock, honey and water. Continue to cook until the carrots are very tender, about 25 minutes.

STRAIN the soup, returning the liquid to the kettle.

IN A food processor or blender purée the vegetables adding just enough of the liquid to aid in the process.

ADD the puréed vegetables to the kettle and return it to a low heat.

ADD the cream and half & half to the soup and bring to a simmer.

ADD the sherry and simmer for 1 to 2 minutes. Adjust the seasoning and serve with a dollop of unsweetened dill whipped cream.

Serves 4-6

Mojito Cheesecake

This is one of the many cheesecakes prepared by Foley Station's Pastry Chef, Jon Hancock. Fashioned after the popular and refreshing South American cocktail by the same name.

Ingredients

For the Topping
1½ cup sour cream
6 tablespoons sugar
2½ tablespoons fresh chopped mint

For the Graham Crust
2 cups graham cracker crumbs
½ cup butter
6 tablespoons brown sugar

For the Filling
1½ pounds cream cheese
½ cup sour cream
1 cup sugar
4 large eggs
1 tablespoon concentrated lime juice
2 tablespoons rum syrup
1 tablespoon dark rum

Preparation

TO PREPARE the crust mixture, place the crumbs and sugar into a bowl. Melt the butter. Add the melted butter, incorporating well.

PRESS the crust evenly into the bottom of a nine-inch cheesecake pan.

BLEND the cream cheese until smooth, scraping the bowl down several times.

ADD sour cream and sugar, continuing to mix. DO NOT WHIP. Incorporating too much air will cause problems in baking.

ADD the eggs, one at a time, mixing well after each addition.

ADD the juice and flavorings. Scrape the bowl. Mix once more then pour over crust into pan.

BAKE at 325 degrees F for 40 minutes.

TURN the oven off and allow the cake to remain in the oven for another hour (Chill before adding topping).

COMBINE the topping ingredients.

POUR over cooled cheesecake.

PLACE in a 400 degree oven for 8 minutes.

CHILL, cut and serve.

Serves 10–12

Baker City posse.

Geiser Grand Hotel

GEISER GRAND
HOTEL

1996 Main St.
Baker City, Oregon
541-523-1889
1-888-GEISERG
www.geisergrand.com

Open 7 days a week
8:00 am – 9:00 pm

Geiser Grand Hotel

Dining room, Geiser Grand Hotel.

The Geiser Grand Hotel and its elegant dining room offer the traveler a chance to step back in time to a level of luxury unprecedented in this area of the country. Baker City is right along the wagon path of the historic Oregon Trail, with the National Historic Oregon Trail Interpretive Center just 5 miles east of the hotel at Flagstaff Hill.

The hotel itself was built in 1889 during a gold mining boom. In its heyday, it was considered to be the finest hotel between Salt Lake City and Seattle. The Geiser family spared no expense in creating a showcase for the wealth they acquired through the Bonanza and other gold mines. The Czechoslovakian architect designed the building using Victorian architecture in the Italianate Renaissance Revival style. It was one of the first hotels in Oregon to offer electricity.

However, when the gold mines closed, economic hard times created a problem for the Geiser Grand. The hotel closed in 1968, shortly after the cast of the movie "Paint Your Wagon" used the hotel while making the movie in the area. Falling into disrepair, the historic old hotel was almost demolished to make way for a parking lot, but was fortunately rescued when a painstaking renovation was begun in 1993. Much of the restoration is original, but other elements were replicated based on painstaking analysis of the building, historical documents and oral history, helping to win an Honor Award for excellence from the National Trust for Historic Preservation.

The beautiful Palm Court dining room features the largest stained glass ceiling in the Pacific Northwest. Rising two stories high, an oval balustrade of cast iron, wrought metal and Honduran mahogany surrounds the Court. One can easily picture Teddy Roosevelt, said to have been a visitor, comfortably sprawled in a dining chair and exhorting his guests about the wonders of the American West.

Today, you can dine in the same room and enjoy the culinary treats of Chef Bill Reichenbach, such as Seafood Pasta, including wild line caught salmon, halibut, shrimp and manila clams, or Mesquite Smoked Prime Rib, followed by one of the many desserts that are made from scratch. Then, walk slowly up the Grand Staircase and enjoy the modern luxury of the renovated rooms, with their silk-damasked draped ten-foot high windows looking out on the beautiful Blue Mountains and the Wallowas.

Geiser Grand Hotel, Baker City

SHIITAKE STEAK

Ingredients

4 8 ounce top sirloin steaks, butterflied
12 ounce shiitake mushrooms, chopped
1 cup sprouts, chopped
1 cup bok choy, chopped
1 tablespoon garlic, minced

1 tablespoon shallots, minced
   salt and pepper to taste
¼ cup while wine
   shiitake demi-glace sauce, see below

Preparation

SAUTÉ the mushrooms, bok choy and red peppers with the garlic and shallots for seven minutes. Salt and pepper to taste. Add white wine, steam for 5 minutes. Remove from heat. Add sprouts to mixture. Divide mixture evenly into the four steaks and close. Bake for 10 minutes in 350° oven. Serve with shiitake demi-glace sauce (below)

For the shiitake demi-glace sauce

NOTE- the home cook may prefer to use a shortcut by purchasing demi-glace powder/mix at specialty food stores; that alternate method is included here.

4 cups demi-glace stock or 1 cup demi-
   glace mix and 32 ounces water
½ cup olive oil

2 cups port wine
5 ounces shiitake mushrooms, julienned

STEAM port wine for 15 minutes. Add demi-glace stock OR add water, bring to boil, add demi-glace mix, stirring constantly. In a separate pan, sauté mushrooms in olive oil. Add to demi-glace.

Northwest Seafood Pasta

Ingredients

3 ounces wild line caught salmon, diced
3 ounces fresh halibut, diced
3 ounces shrimp, peeled and smoked
3 ounces manila clams, steamed,
  de-shelled
1 tablespoon fresh basil, minced
1 tablespoon garlic, minced
1 tablespoon shallots, minced

salt and pepper to taste
2 tablespoons olive oil
⅛ cup white wine
2 cups good tomato sauce
8 ounces linguine noodles
fresh vine ripened tomato, diced
fresh parsley, chopped

Preparation

IN A saucepan simmer olive oil, garlic, shallots, basil, over low heat add shrimp, halibut and salmon. Cook for 4 minutes. Add white wine and steam for 2 minutes. Add tomato sauce, salt, pepper. Cook for 5 minutes. Serve over linguine cooked al dente; top with steamed clams. GARNISH with fresh tomatoes and parsley.

Geiser Grand Saloon.

Geiser Grand Hotel, Baker City

CHOCOLATE HAZELNUT TORTE

Ingredients

For the Filling
- ½ cup granulated sugar
- ¼ cup water
- ¼ cup Frangelico (hazelnut liqueur)
- 1 cup butter (2 sticks)
- 1 cup cream
- ¼ cup honey
- 2½ cups toasted hazelnuts, skinned and chopped

Dark Chocolate Ganache Topping
- 8 ounces bittersweet chocolate, chopped
- 8 ounces semi-sweet chocolate, chopped
- 4 ounces white chocolate, chopped
- 2½ cups cream

For the Cake
- 1½ cups toasted hazelnuts, skinned
- 1 cup sugar
- 6 ounces bittersweet chocolate
- 6 ounces semi-sweet chocolate
- 2 ounces white chocolate
- ¾ cup unsalted butter, room temperature
- 8 eggs, separated
- 2 teaspoons vanilla
- ½ cup all-purpose flour
- ½ teaspoon salt
- ½ teaspoon cream of tartar

Preparation

For Filling
IN A small, heavy bottomed saucepan, combine sugar, water, and Frangelico. Heat over medium-high heat until the mixture turns a light amber color. Add butter and cream and simmer for 15 minutes Take off the heat and stir in honey and the chopped hazelnuts. Allow to cool completely.

For the Cake
PREHEAT oven to 375 degrees. Butter the sides and bottom of two 9-inch, spring form pans and line the bottoms with parchment or waxed paper.

IN THE bowl of a food processor, chop the hazelnuts finely with 4 tablespoons of sugar. Set aside.

IN THE top of a double boiler, melt the chocolates with the softened butter. Stir until smooth.

IN A bowl, whisk egg yolks with ⅔ cup sugar. Stir in chocolate mixture and vanilla.

MIX the flour and salt with the hazelnuts and fold into the chocolate mixture

IN A large bowl, beat the egg whites with cream of tarter until soft peaks form. Add the remaining sugar and beat until the whites are stiff but not dry, Fold a spoonful of the egg whites into the chocolate mixture (to lighten it). Then carefully fold in the remaining egg white mixture. Divide the batter into 2 prepared pans. Bake for 30-35 minutes Cool completely on wire racks,

For the Dark Ganache

IN A saucepan, heat cream until bubbles begin to form around the edges. Place the chopped chocolate in a bowl and pour the hot cream over the chocolate. Let sit for 5 minutes. Stir to ensure the chocolate is melted and smooth Allow to cool to room temperature.

Assembly

AFTER the cakes are cool, set them on a table and trim the tops so they are flat. Spread the hazelnut filling on the top of the bottom cake. Place the second cake or top of the filling and press gently.

PLACE the cake on a wire rack with a baking pan or cookie sheet under to catch the excess ganache. Pour the dark chocolate ganache over the top of the cake slowly covering all of the cake. (The ganache should be pourable. Re-warm slightly, if needed). Use a rubber spatula to guide the ganache into any openings on the sides of the cake. Decorate with chocolate curls and whole hazelnuts. Chill on wire racks for 4 hours

Makes 1 9-inch torte

Early Oregon rodeo.

OREGON SPIRIT IN A BOTTLE

It takes 28 pounds of fresh Oregon pears to make a single large bottle of Clear Creek Distillery's Pear Brandy.

Clear Creek's brandies are based on the classic Eau-de-Vie de poire. "Eau-de-Vie' literally means "water of life." The process is less scientific than it is folklore, according to Steve McCarthy, the master distiller and founder of this Portland-based company. McCarthy traveled thoroughout Europe to learn the traditional methods of making this clear fruit-based spirit, listening to stories handed down from generation to generation of farmers, telling of timing, method, and manner for producing a fine fruit brandy. McCarthy combined the techniques he learned with the outstanding fruit from his own Oregon orchards, launching the Clear Creek Distillery in 1987.

Starting with quality fruit is a large part of the success of Clear Creek's products. The end result relies completely on the pears selected. Understanding the timing and creating the proper environment are additional factors critical to the outcome.

McCarthy has the knack. In 1994, the New York Time Magazine said "… Steve McCarthy's Clear Creek Distillery is producing what many experts feel to be the best fruit brandies (pear, raspberry, apple) ever made in the U.S." At the World Spirits Competition held in San Francisco in 2000, Clear Creek Distillery was awarded a double gold medal.

Perhaps the most distinctive product is the "Pear-In-A-Bottle," which requires the distillery crew to painstakingly encase individual flowering tree limbs in sterilized bottles, and secure the container to hang in such a way the pear can continue to develop inside the glass. This procedure is done in May and takes nearly two weeks to complete, culminating in a couple hundred cases worth of bottled pears.

Clear Creek makes eau-de-vie entirely from Oregon fruit, using traditional European pot stills, along with techniques learned in Alsace and Switzerland. The distinctive "nose", or initial scent, comes from careful fermentation and distillation. The taste is simply the clear and fiery essence of the fruit. No colors, sugars, or flavors are ever added.

Connoisseurs and the curious should not miss the chance to see where this delightful spirit is created. Call 503-248-9470 to make an appointment to visit Clear Creek Distillery, located in the Northwest/Nob Hill neighborhood of Portland.

And, Bon Appetite!

CULINARY SOURCES

DAIRY

Tillamook Creamery
Tillamook cheese, ice cream, butter, milk, sour cream.
4175 Highway 101 North
P.O. Box 313
Tillamook, Oregon 97141
Phone: 503-815-1300
www.tillamookcheese.com

The Rogue Creamery
Oregon Rogue River Blue Cheese
311 N. Front Street
Central Point, OR 97502
Phone: 866-665-1155
Phone: 541-665-1155
Fax: 541-665-1133
www.roguegoldcheese.com

FISH AND SEAFOOD

Gerard & Dominique Seafood
European and Northwest style smoked salmon, seafood sausage and smoked scallops.
P.O. Box 1845
Bothell, Washington 98041
Phone: 800-858-0449
Fax: 425-488-9229
www.gdseafoods.com

Taylor Shellfish Farms, Inc.
Clams, oysters, mussels, and geoduck.
130 SE Lynch Road
Shelton, WA 98585
Phone: 360-425-6178
Fax: 360-427-0327
www.taylorshellfish.com

The Freshest Seafood
Complete selection of fresh seafood, truffles and Tobikko caviar
1111 NW 45st Suite B
Seattle, WA 98107
Phone: 877-706-4022
www.seafoodfoodsuperstore.com
email info@simplyseafood.com

FRUIT

Pear Bureau Northwest
All about pears
4382 SE International Way Ste A
Milwaukie, OR 97222-4635
Phone: 503-652-9720
Phone: 503-652-9721
www.usapears.com

KITCHEN ACCESSORIES & SUPPLIES

Cooks, Pots and Tabletops
2807 Oak St.
Eugene, OR 97405
(541) 338-4339
Fax: (541) 338-4339

Kitchen Kaboodle
Cookware, kitchenware, dinnerware, furniture and accessories for the home.
535 S.W. 6th Ave.
Portland, Oregon 97208
Phone: 503-464-9545
www.kitchenkaboodle.com

Lullu's Tutto Cucina
Cooking classes, specialty
import items (especially Italian)
357 Court St. NE
Salem, OR 97301
Phone: (503) 364-7900
Fax: (503) 364-7901
www.tuttocucina.org
Email: lullu@tuttocucina.org

MUSHROOMS

Gourmet Mushroom Products
Mushrooms and truffle oils
P.O. Box 515 IP
Graton, CA 9544
Phone: 800-789-9121
www.gmushrooms.com

NUTS AND TRUFFLES

Hazelnut Marketing Board
21595-A Dolores Way NE
Aurora, OR 97002-9738
Phone: 503-678-6823
Phone: 503-678-6825
www.oregonhazelnuts.com

The Northwest Products Store
Selections of berries, hazelnuts and more.
Corporate Office: 31461 NE Bell Road
Sherwood, OR 97140
Phone: 503-554-9060
Fax: 503-537-9693
Toll Free: 888-252-0699
www.yournw.com

The Truffle Market
Truffles
P.O. Box 4234
Gettysburg, PA 17325
Phone: 800-822-4003
www.trufflemarket.com

SPICES

Penzeys Spices
Complete selection of spices
19300 West Janacek Court
P.O. Box 924
Brookfield, WI 53308
Phone: 800-741-7787
www.penzeys.com

SPIRITS AND WINE

Clear Creek Distillery
Pure fruit spirits from Oregon fruit.
1430 NW 23rd Ave.
Portland, OR 97210
Phone: 503-248-9470
www.clearcreekdistillery.com

Mead is available through:
http://medovina.com or,
www.redstonemeadery.com

WILD GAME AND MEAT

Antelope, buffalo, wild boar, alligator
Seattle's Finest Exotic Meats
Phone: 800-680-4375
www.exoticmeats.com

Nicky Game USA
223 SE 3rd Avenue
Portland, OR 97214
Phone: 503-234-4263
Phone: 800-469-4162
Fax: 503-234-8268
www.nickyusawildgame.com

Carlton Farms
High Quality Gourmet Meats; Bacon, Ham, Pork Chops, Pork Sausage, Country style ribs, Tenderloins
P.O. Box 580
Carlton, OR 97111
Phone: 800-932-0946
Phone: 503-852-7166
www.carltonfarms.com

Valley Game & Gourmet
Specializing in wild game & gourmet pantry items
P.O. Box 2713
Salt Lake City, UT 84110
Phone: 800-521-2156
Phone: 801-521-2345
www.valleygame.com

Oakwood Game Farms
Fresh & smoked pheasants, chukar partridge, quail, duck, also wild rice
P.O. Box 274
Princeton, MN 55371
Phone: 800-328-6647
www.oakwoodgamefarm.com

Prairie Harvest Specialty Foods
Buffalo, elk, venison, wild boar, rabbit, pheasant, quail, duck, goose; mushrooms, berries, and Foie Gras
P.O. Box 1013
Spearfish, SD 57783
www.prairieharvest.com

Broken Arrow Ranch
Antelope, Venison, wild boar
P.O. Box 530, Ingram, TX 78025
Phone: 800-962-4263
www.brokenarrowranch.com

MISCELLANEOUS

The Next Day Gourmet
Fast delivery for specialty foods (prepared cannoli shells, pastas, etc.) and kitchen tools
www.nextdaygourmet.com

Directory of Farmer's Markets, by state
www.ams.usda.gov/farmers-markets/maps.htm

Wine & Farm Tour
Visit an Oregon farm or winery and experience Oregon's agriculture culture and lifestyle.
www.oregonfarmtours.com

Made In Oregon
P.O. Box 3458
Portland, Oregon 97208-9936
Phone: 503-273-8719
Phone: 800-828-9673
Fax: 503-222-6855
www.madeinoregon.com

The ultimate source for culinary questions, definitions, and recipes
www.epicurious.com

Glossary

aioli	A mayonnaise strongly seasoned with garlic or other seasoning.
bain-marie	A term indicating a container placed inside another container of water so the food cooks gently
béarnaise sauce	A classic French sauce made with vinegar, wine, tarragon, and shallots, reduced and finished with egg yolks and butter.
beurre blanc	"White butter," this sauce is composed of wine, vinegar, shallots and butter.
blanch	Plunging food (usually vegetables and fruits) into boiling water briefly, then into cold water to stop the cooking process.
braise	Browning food (usually meat or vegetables) first in fat, then cooking in a small amount of liquid, covered, at low heat for a long time.
brown sauce	A sauce traditionally made of a rich meat stock.
capers	The flower bud of a bush native to the Mediterranean and parts of Asia, picked, sun-dried, and then pickled.
chèvre cheese	French for "goat," chèvre is a pure white goat's-milk cheese with a tart flavor.
chiffonade	Similar to julienne, the process of cutting lettuce, endive, or herbs into thin, even strips.
chipotle	A dried, smoked, Jalapeno with a sweet, almost chocolaty flavor.
clarified	The process of clearing a cloudy substance, such as in stocks or wines, or melting butter until the foam rises and is skimmed off.
clementine mandarin	The clementine is a hybrid variety of tangerine.
confectioners' sugar	Powdered sugar.
court bullion	A poaching liquid usually made up of vegetables, water, herbs and wine or vinegar.
crème anglaise	A cooked mixture of cream, sugar, egg yolks, and usually vanilla for flavoring.
crème fraîche	A thick, velvety cream that can be boiled without curdling.
crostini	Small, thin slices of toasted bread, usually brushed with olive oil.
de-bearding	To pull the threads towards the hinge of the mussel and tear out.
daikon	A large Asian radish with a sweet, fresh flavor.
demi-glace	A rich brown sauce (usually meat stock) combined with Madeira or sherry and slowly cooked until it's reduced by half to a thick glaze.
deglaze	Adding wine or water to the skillet to loosen browned bits on the bottom to make a sauce.
demi-sec	In cooking, it refers to reducing by half. In wine, it refers to the level of sweetness.

foie gras	The term generally used for goose liver.
frenched	To trim fat or bone from a cut of meat.
grappa	A colorless, high alcohol Italian spirit distilled from the grape skins and seeds remaining in the wine press after the wine has been made.
gratinée	To brown (usually crumbs and butter) under a broiler or with a torch.
gremulata	A garnish made of minced parsley, lemon peel, and garlic.
julienne	A method of cutting vegetables into thin strips, usually about 1 inch by $\frac{1}{16}$ inch.
kosher salt	An additive-free coarse-grained salt.
macerate	To soak a food (usually fruit) in a liquid so it absorbs the flavor.
Madeira	Madeira is a distinctive fortified wine and is an excellent cooking wine.
mascarpone	An Italian cream cheese; double- to triple-rich and buttery.
mead	Fermented honey, water and yeast with flavorings of spices, herbs and flowers.
mesclun	A mix of young, small salad greens, such as arugula, dandelion and radicchio.
meunière	Lightly dusting a meat or fish in flour and sautéing in butter, usually with lemon juice sprinkled on top.
mirepoix; mirepois	A mixture of diced carrots, onions, celery and herbs sautéed in butter.
mise en place	To have all the ingredients necessary for a dish and be ready to combine for cooking.
morel mushroom	An edible wild mushroom belonging to the same fungus species as the truffle.
mirin	A sweet, rice wine used in cooking to sweeten meat or fish dishes.
napoleon	A dish made with a variety of layers, usually a dessert.
nappe	Usually referring to a coating, such as a sauce thick enough to coat a spoon.
paella	A Spanish rice dish with meats, shellfish, or vegetables, usually flavored with saffron.
pancetta	Slightly salty Italian bacon cured with salt and spices, but not smoked.
panko	Coarse bread crumbs (Japanese) used for coating fried foods.
prosciutto	Italian word for ham; seasoned, salt-cured and air-dried, but not smoked.
purée	To grind or mash food until it's completely smooth, using a food processor, a blender, or by forcing the food through a sieve.
ragout	A stew made of meats or vegetables, well seasoned and thickened.
ramekin	An individual earthenware-baking dish similar to a miniature soufflé dish.
reduce (reduction)	To boil a liquid rapidly, reducing it until its thickened and flavorful.
render	To convert or melt down fat by slow heating.
ribbon stage	The stage in a recipe when the ingredients thicken enough to flow from your whisk or spoon in a continuous ribbon.

roux	A mixture of equal parts flour and butter used to thicken sauces. Cooking different lengths of time results in different flavors and colors.
sauté	To quickly cook food over direct heat in a small amount of hot oil.
sec	This French word means "dry".
shallot	Member of the onion family.
steep	To soak dry ingredients in liquid until the flavor is absorbed by the liquid.
sweat	To cook vegetables slowly in their own juices.
tapenade	A spread or condiment, usually consisting of puréed capers, olives, and anchovies in olive oil.
tartare	Often refers to a raw meat dish.
temper	To warm beaten eggs, by stirring a little of the hot ingredients into them, before adding the hot ingredients in entirety, so the eggs don't solidify.
truffle	A fungus that is cultivated primarily in France and Italy, valued for its earthy, aromatic nature.
truffle oil	Truffle oil is created when truffles are soaked in olive oil.
tuile	A flavored thin, crisp cookie that is usually curved.
U-15 shrimp	Pertains to the size of the shrimp; the number following the U denotes the approximate number of shrimp per pound.
velouté	A stock-based white sauce, used as a base for other sauces.
Viognier; Vionnier	Intense, dry white wines with vibrant floral qualities and an intriguing bouquet with hints of apricots, peaches, and pears.
wilted spinach/ lettuce	Wilting spinach or lettuce, by steaming or drizzling hot liquid over them.
Zabaglione	A custard-like dessert made by whisking together egg yolks, wine and sugar.
zest	The brightly colored outermost skin layer of citrus fruit, removed with a zester, grater, or knife.

About the Publishers

Chuck and Blanche Johnson started Wilderness Adventures Press, Inc. in 1993, publishing outdoor and sporting books. Along with hunting and fishing, they love fine dining, good wines, and traveling. They have always been able to "sniff out" the most outstanding and interesting restaurants in any city they visit.

On weekends, they experiment in the kitchen, cooking a variety of fish and meats, as well as preparing the harvest from their time in the field. This love of cooking has resulted in a large library of cookbooks, and has inspired them to create a series of cookbooks based on their love of travel and fine dining.

Chuck and Blanche make their home in Gallatin Gateway, Montana, along with their four German wirehaired pointers.

Photo Copyrights/Credits

Cover, left to right accross: ©Columbia Gorge Hotel; ©Columbia Gorge Hotel; ©Cork; ©Chives; ©Columbia Gorge Hotel; ©Marche; ©Douglas County Museum; ©Big River Restaurant; ©Baker City Museum; ©Silver Salmon Grille; ©Dundee Bistro; ©Douglas County Museum. **Back cover left to right accross:** ©Caruso's Italian Cafe; ©Hood River Hotel; ©Lord Bennett's; ©Chives; ©Marche; ©Monet. **i:** ©Douglas County Museum. **iii-vii:** ©Art Today. **viii-large:** ©Hood River County Historical Museum; ©. **viii-small:** ©Clatsop County Historical Society. **x:** ©Clatsop County Historical Society. **xiv:** ©Clatsop County Historical Society. **1-5:** ©Chives Restaurant. **7, 8, 10:** ©Lord Bennett's. **11, 12, 14:** ©Salishan Lodge. **17:** ©Art Today. **18:** Bay House. **24:** ©Clatsop County Historical Society. **24, 25, 29:** ©Stephanie Inn. **30:** ©Clatsop County Historical Society. **31, 32:** ©Silver Salmon Grille. **38:** ©Clatsop County Historical Society. **39, 40, 44:** ©Dundee Bistro. **45:** ©Art Today. **46:** ©Caruso's Italian Cafe. **51:** ©Art Today. **52:** ©Rose of Sharon. **56:** ©Douglas County Museum. **57, 58:** ©Silver Grille. **61:** ©Frank Barnett. **62-top:** ©Art Today. **62-bottom:** ©J James Restaurant. **66:** ©Springfield Museum. **67:** ©Blanche Johnson. **68:** ©Morton's Bistro. **73, 74:** ©Frank Barnett. **77, 78:** ©Big River Restaurant. **86:** ©Hood River County Historical Museum. **87:** ©Blanche Johnson. **88, 91:** ©Le Bistro. **93:** ©Blanche Johnson. **94, 96, 97:** ©Adam's Place. **98:** ©Douglas County Historical Society. **99:** ©Blanche Johnson. **100, 104:** ©Chanterelle. **105, 106, 110:** ©Marché. **113, 114, 118:** ©Sweet Waters. **119:** ©Blanche Johnson. **120:** ©Willies. **123:** ©Clatsop County Historical Society. **124:** ©Douglas County Museum. **125, 126, 130:** ©Steamboat Inn. **131, 132, 138:** ©Morrison's Rogue River Lodge. **140:** ©Douglas County Museum. **141, 142, 145:** ©Jacksonville Inn. **149:** ©Blanche Johnson. **150:** ©Douglas County Museum. **155, 156:** ©Blanche Johnson. **157, 158:** ©Monet. **164:** ©Blanche Johnson. **165, 166, 168, 170:** ©Broken Top Club. **171, 172:** ©Cork. **176, 178:** ©Blanche Johnson. **177, 181:** ©Columbia Gorge Hotel. **183:** ©Blanche Johnson. **184, 186:** ©Hood River Hotel. **188:** ©Hood River County Historical Museum. **189:** ©Art Today. **190, 192:** ©Stonehedge Gardens. **195:** ©Hood River County Historical Museum. **196:** ©Hood River County Historical Museum. **200:** ©Hood River County Historical Museum. **201, 202:** ©Hotel Condon. **207:** ©Raphael's. **208, 212:** ©Art Today. **213, 214:** ©Foley Station. **220:** ©Baker City Museum. **221, 222, 224:** Geizer Grand. **226:** Douglas County Historical Society.

INDEX